Supporting Your Child: Practical Tips For Parenting Kids With ADHD

Odedra Kiran

Published by Odedra Kiran, 2024.

SUPPORTING YOUR CHILD: PRACTICAL TIPS FOR PARENTING KIDS WITH ADHD

First edition. March 30, 2024.

Copyright © 2024 Odedra Kiran.

ISBN: 979-8224211784

Written by Odedra Kiran.

Table of Contents

Chapter 1: Understanding ADHD

- WHAT IS ADHD?

Attention-deficit/hyperactivity disorder, commonly known as ADHD, is a neurodevelopmental disorder that affects both children and adults. It is characterized by a persistent pattern of inattention and/or hyperactivity-impulsivity that interferes with daily functioning or development. Symptoms of ADHD can vary depending on the individual and may present differently in children versus adults. In children, symptoms may include difficulty paying attention, impulsive behavior, and hyperactivity, while in adults, symptoms may manifest as disorganization, forgetfulness, and difficulty completing tasks.

ADHD is one of the most common mental health disorders affecting children, with an estimated 5-7% of school-aged children diagnosed with the disorder. While ADHD is often diagnosed in childhood, it can also persist into adulthood, with an estimated 2. 5% of adults in the United States living with the disorder. It is important to note that ADHD is not a result of laziness, lack of motivation, or poor parenting, but rather a complex neurobiological condition that is influenced by genetic, environmental, and developmental factors.

The exact cause of ADHD is not fully understood, but research suggests that a combination of genetic and environmental factors play a role in the development of the disorder. Studies have shown that individuals with a family history of ADHD are more likely to develop the disorder themselves, indicating a strong genetic component. Additionally, certain environmental factors, such as exposure to tobacco smoke during pregnancy, premature birth, and low birth weight, have been linked to an increased risk of developing ADHD.

Diagnosing ADHD can be challenging, as there is no definitive test or biomarker for the disorder. Instead, clinicians rely on a comprehensive evaluation that may include a thorough medical history, physical examination, and assessment of symptoms and behaviors. The Diagnostic and Statistical Manual of Mental Disorders (DSM-5) outlines specific criteria for diagnosing ADHD, which include persistent patterns of inattention, hyperactivity, and impulsivity that significantly impair functioning in multiple settings.

Treatment for ADHD often involves a combination of medication, behavioral therapy, and education and support services. Stimulant medications, such as methylphenidate and amphetamine, are commonly prescribed to help manage symptoms of inattention, hyperactivity, and impulsivity. Behavioral therapy, such as cognitive-behavioral therapy (CBT) and parent training, can also be effective in helping individuals with ADHD develop coping skills and strategies for managing their symptoms. Additionally, education and support services, such as academic accommodations and psychoeducation, can help individuals with ADHD succeed in school, work, and social settings. While the exact cause of ADHD is not fully understood, research suggests that genetic and environmental factors play a role in the development of the disorder. Diagnosing ADHD can be challenging, but a comprehensive evaluation that considers a person's medical history, symptoms, and behaviors can help identify the presence of the disorder. Treatment for ADHD often involves a combination of medication, behavioral therapy, and education and support services to help individuals manage their symptoms and improve their quality of life. By raising awareness and understanding of ADHD, we can better support individuals living with the disorder and promote their mental health and well-being.

- Common symptoms of ADHD

Attention Deficit Hyperactivity Disorder, commonly known as ADHD, is a neurodevelopmental disorder that affects both children and adults. It is characterized by a persistent pattern of inattention, hyperactivity, and impulsivity that interferes with daily functioning. While the exact cause of ADHD is still unknown, research suggests that genetic factors, brain structure, and environmental influences may all play a role in the development of the disorder.

One of the most common symptoms of ADHD is inattention. Individuals with ADHD often have difficulty staying focused on tasks or activities, making careless mistakes, and organizing their thoughts or belongings. They may also struggle with following instructions, listening attentively, and completing tasks that require sustained mental effort. Inattention symptoms can vary in severity and may manifest differently in different individuals.

Hyperactivity is another key symptom of ADHD. People with ADHD may be constantly on the go, fidgeting or squirming in their seats, and talking excessively. They may have difficulty sitting still for long periods of time and may engage in impulsive behaviors without considering the consequences. Hyperactivity symptoms can be especially disruptive in school or work settings, where individuals are expected to sit still and focus on specific tasks.

Impulsivity is a third hallmark symptom of ADHD. Individuals with ADHD may act without thinking, blurting out answers to questions before they are fully asked or interrupting others during conversations. They may have difficulty waiting their turn or controlling their emotions, leading to impulsive or risky behaviors. Impulsivity can have serious consequences, such as accidents, conflicts with others, or poor decision-making.

Other common symptoms of ADHD include forgetfulness, disorganization, and difficulty with time management. People with ADHD may frequently lose items, forget appointments, or have difficulty keeping track of deadlines. They may also struggle with prioritizing tasks, managing their time effectively, and staying on schedule. These symptoms can lead to academic or occupational challenges, as well as interpersonal difficulties with friends, family, and colleagues.

It is important to note that the symptoms of ADHD can vary widely from person to person. Some individuals may primarily struggle with inattention, while others may exhibit more prominent hyperactivity or impulsivity. Additionally, the severity of symptoms can fluctuate over time, depending on factors such as stress, fatigue, or changes in routine. It is also possible for individuals to have co-occurring conditions, such as anxiety, depression, or learning disabilities, which can further complicate the presentation of ADHD symptoms.

Diagnosing ADHD involves a comprehensive evaluation by a qualified healthcare provider, typically a psychiatrist, psychologist, or primary care physician. The diagnostic process may include a review of the individual's medical history, a physical examination, and interviews with the individual and their family members. Standardized rating scales and behavioral assessments may also be used to gather information about the individual's symptoms and functional impairments.

Treatment for ADHD often involves a combination of medication, behavior therapy, and lifestyle modifications. Stimulant medications, such as methylphenidate or amphetamines, are commonly prescribed to help improve attention, focus, and impulse control. Non-stimulant medications, such as atomoxetine or guanfacine, may also be used in some cases. Behavioral interventions, such as cognitive-behavioral therapy or parent training, can help individuals develop coping strategies and improve their organizational and time-management skills. By recognizing the common symptoms of ADHD, seeking a comprehensive evaluation, and developing a personalized treatment plan, individuals with ADHD can learn to manage their symptoms effectively and lead fulfilling and productive lives. With the right support and resources, it is possible to thrive with ADHD and reach one's full potential.

- Types of ADHD

Attention-deficit/hyperactivity disorder (ADHD) is a neurodevelopmental disorder that affects both children and adults. ADHD is characterized by a persistent pattern of inattention, hyperactivity, and impulsivity that can impact various aspects of a person's life, such as academic and work performance, social interactions, and emotional well-being. There are three main types of ADHD that are commonly diagnosed: inattentive type, hyperactive-impulsive type, and combined type. Each type presents with its own set of symptoms and challenges, but all can be effectively managed with appropriate treatment and support.

The inattentive type of ADHD is characterized by difficulty paying attention, following instructions, and staying organized. Individuals with this type of ADHD may frequently lose or forget things, have trouble completing tasks, and struggle to sustain mental effort for extended periods of time. They may also appear forgetful, easily distracted, and disorganized in their daily lives.

While they may not display the hyperactive or impulsive behaviors typically associated with ADHD, they still experience significant impairments in their ability to focus and concentrate on tasks.

On the other hand, the hyperactive-impulsive type of ADHD is characterized by a constant state of restlessness, fidgeting, and impulsivity. Individuals with this type of ADHD may have difficulty sitting still, waiting their turn, or engaging in activities quietly. They may also interrupt conversations, act impulsively without considering the consequences, and have difficulty controlling their impulses. While they may have fewer problems with inattention, their hyperactive and impulsive behaviors can still seriously interfere with their daily functioning and relationships.

The combined type of ADHD is the most common presentation and is characterized by a combination of inattentive, hyperactive, and impulsive symptoms. Individuals with this type of ADHD exhibit a diverse range of symptoms that can vary in severity and presentation. They may struggle with both attention and executive functioning skills, such as planning, organizing, and prioritizing tasks. They may also have difficulty regulating their emotions and behaviors, leading to challenges in social interactions and self-control. This combination of symptoms can make it especially challenging for individuals with combined-type ADHD to manage their daily responsibilities and relationships.

While each type of ADHD has its own unique set of symptoms, it is important to recognize that ADHD is a complex and heterogeneous disorder that can manifest differently in each individual. Some people may exhibit predominantly inattentive symptoms, while others may display more hyperactive-impulsive symptoms. Additionally, symptoms can change over time and may be influenced by various factors, such as stress, sleep, and environmental triggers. It is crucial to conduct a comprehensive evaluation and assessment to accurately diagnose and differentiate the various types of ADHD, as well as to tailor treatment interventions to address the specific needs and challenges of each individual.

Treatment for ADHD typically involves a multimodal approach that combines medication, behavioral interventions, and psychosocial support. Stimulant medications, such as methylphenidate and amphetamine-based drugs, are commonly prescribed to help manage symptoms of inattention, hyperactivity, and impulsivity. These medications work by increasing the levels of neurotransmitters in the brain that are involved in regulating attention, focus, and impulse control. However, medication alone is not always sufficient to address the complex and multifaceted nature of ADHD. Behavioral interventions, such as cognitive-behavioral therapy, parent training, and social skills training, are also important components of a comprehensive treatment plan. These interventions can help individuals develop coping strategies, improve executive functioning skills, and enhance their self-regulation abilities.

In addition to medication and behavioral interventions, psychosocial support and accommodations are essential for individuals with ADHD to thrive in various settings, such as school, work, and social environments. Educational accommodations, such as extended time on tests, preferential seating, and individualized learning plans, can help students with ADHD succeed academically. Workplace accommodations, such as flexible schedules, structured tasks, and quiet workspaces, can also support adults with ADHD in achieving their professional goals. Furthermore, psychoeducation, support groups, and coaching services can provide individuals with ADHD and their families with valuable information, resources, and guidance on how to effectively manage the challenges of the disorder. The three main types of ADHD – inattentive type, hyperactive-impulsive type, and combined type – each present with their own set of symptoms and challenges. It is important to conduct a thorough evaluation and assessment to accurately diagnose and differentiate the various types of ADHD, as well as to develop a personalized treatment plan that addresses the specific needs and challenges of each individual. By combining medication, behavioral interventions, and psychosocial support, individuals with ADHD can effectively manage their symptoms and improve their overall functioning and quality of life.

Chapter 2: Diagnosing ADHD

- THE DIAGNOSTIC PROCESS

The diagnostic process is a crucial step in the field of medicine that involves identifying and determining the nature of a patient's illness or condition. It is a complex and intricate procedure that requires the collaboration of various healthcare professionals, including doctors, nurses, radiologists, and laboratory technicians. The ultimate goal of the diagnostic process is to provide a definitive diagnosis for a patient's symptoms, which enables healthcare providers to develop an appropriate treatment plan.

The diagnostic process typically begins with a thorough evaluation of the patient's medical history and symptoms. This information is collected through interviews with the patient, as well as examinations and tests conducted by healthcare professionals. The next step in the diagnostic process is to perform various diagnostic tests, such as blood tests, imaging studies, and biopsies, to gather further information about the patient's condition. These tests allow healthcare providers to obtain detailed data about the patient's health and help to confirm or rule out potential diagnoses.

One key component of the diagnostic process is the differential diagnosis, which involves considering all possible causes of a patient's symptoms and systematically narrowing down the potential diagnoses based on clinical findings and test results. This process requires healthcare providers to use their medical knowledge and expertise to critically analyze the available information and arrive at a final diagnosis. In some cases, healthcare providers may need to consult with specialists or refer the patient to a specialized clinic for further evaluation and testing.

It is important to note that the diagnostic process is not always straightforward, and there can be challenges and uncertainties along the way. Some conditions may present with vague or atypical symptoms, making them difficult to diagnose. In addition, patients may have multiple underlying health issues or complex medical histories that can complicate the diagnostic process. Healthcare providers must remain vigilant and open-minded during the diagnostic process, considering all possible explanations and seeking additional information as needed.

In recent years, advances in medical technology and diagnostic tools have revolutionized the diagnostic process, making it more efficient and accurate. Techniques such as genetic testing, molecular diagnostics, and advanced imaging modalities have enabled healthcare providers to identify diseases at an earlier stage and with greater precision. These technological advancements have also improved the ability to tailor treatment plans to individual patients, leading to better outcomes and reduced healthcare costs. It requires a multidisciplinary approach, with healthcare providers working together to collect and interpret data, reach a final diagnosis, and develop a comprehensive treatment plan. By staying informed of the latest advancements in diagnostic technology and approaches, healthcare providers can continue to improve the accuracy and efficiency of the diagnostic process, ultimately leading to better patient outcomes and quality of care.

- Who can diagnose ADHD?

Attention Deficit Hyperactivity Disorder (ADHD) is a common neurodevelopmental disorder that affects both children and adults. The diagnosis of ADHD requires a comprehensive evaluation by a trained healthcare professional, such as a psychiatrist, psychologist, pediatrician, or neurologist. These professionals have the necessary expertise and experience to accurately assess and diagnose ADHD based on established diagnostic criteria. While teachers, parents, and other individuals may observe symptoms of ADHD in a person, only qualified healthcare professionals can provide a formal diagnosis.

ADHD is characterized by persistent patterns of inattention, hyperactivity, and impulsivity that can significantly impact an individual's daily functioning and quality of life. In order to determine whether the symptoms are indicative of ADHD, a thorough assessment is necessary. This typically involves gathering information from multiple sources, including a detailed medical history, observations of the individual's behavior in different settings, standardized rating scales, and potentially, psychological testing. The diagnostic process may also include ruling out other potential explanations for the symptoms, such as anxiety disorders, learning disabilities, or mood disorders.

Healthcare professionals who diagnose ADHD follow guidelines established by organizations such as the American Psychiatric Association (APA) and the American Academy of Pediatrics (AAP). These guidelines outline specific criteria that must be met in order to make a formal diagnosis of ADHD. For children, the DSM-5 criteria are typically used, which include symptoms of inattention, hyperactivity, and impulsivity that are present in multiple settings and interfere with the individual's functioning. In adults, the criteria are similar but may manifest differently due to the developmental differences between children and adults.

One of the key components of an ADHD assessment is obtaining information from multiple sources, such as parents, teachers, and other caregivers. This is important because symptoms of ADHD may vary depending on the setting and may not be readily apparent during a brief office visit. By gathering information from multiple sources, healthcare professionals can gain a more comprehensive understanding of the individual's behavior and functioning. In some cases, collateral information may also be obtained from academic records, medical records, or other relevant sources to help inform the diagnosis.

In addition to gathering information from multiple sources, healthcare professionals may also use standardized rating scales to help assess symptoms of ADHD. These scales are completed by parents, teachers, and sometimes the individual themselves, and provide valuable information about the severity and frequency of symptoms. While rating scales are not a definitive diagnostic tool on their own, they can be a helpful supplement to the clinical assessment process. Psychological testing may also be used in some cases to further clarify the diagnosis, particularly if there are concerns about co-occurring conditions or difficulties with learning or memory.

It is important to note that a diagnosis of ADHD should not be made hastily or based solely on one observation or piece of information. The diagnostic process for ADHD is complex and requires careful consideration of multiple factors. Healthcare professionals who specialize in ADHD have the training and expertise to evaluate the full range of symptoms and develop an appropriate treatment plan. This may include medication, therapy, behavioral interventions, and accommodations to help the individual manage their symptoms and improve their functioning. These professionals use established diagnostic criteria, gather information from multiple sources, and may use standardized rating scales or psychological testing to help clarify the diagnosis. By following a comprehensive assessment process, healthcare professionals can provide an accurate diagnosis of ADHD and develop a personalized treatment plan to help individuals manage their symptoms and improve their quality of life. It is important to seek help from a qualified professional if you suspect that you or someone you know may have ADHD, as early intervention and treatment can make a significant difference in outcomes and overall well-being.

- Understanding a diagnosis

Understanding a diagnosis is a crucial aspect of healthcare that affects both patients and healthcare providers. A diagnosis is a medical determination of the cause of an individual's symptoms or health issues. It is typically made by a healthcare professional, such as a doctor or specialist, after a thorough evaluation of the patient's medical history, symptoms, and diagnostic tests. The diagnostic process is essential for guiding treatment decisions and determining the prognosis for the patient's condition.

When a patient receives a diagnosis, it can bring a sense of relief by providing an explanation for their symptoms and validating their concerns. However, it can also be overwhelming and confusing, especially if the diagnosis is complex or unfamiliar. Patients may have questions about their condition, its causes, treatment options, and long-term implications. It is important for healthcare providers to communicate clearly and effectively with patients to help them understand their diagnosis and make informed decisions about their care.

Healthcare providers play a crucial role in helping patients understand their diagnosis. They must explain the medical terminology in simple terms and provide information about the condition, its causes, and treatment options. Providers should encourage patients to ask questions and express their concerns, and they should also offer support and reassurance during the diagnostic process. Additionally, healthcare providers should involve patients in decision-making regarding their care, taking into account their preferences, values, and goals.

In addition to communicating with patients, healthcare providers must also work collaboratively with other members of the healthcare team to ensure a comprehensive understanding of the diagnosis and a coordinated approach to treatment. This may involve consulting with specialists, ordering additional tests or imaging studies, or seeking a second opinion to confirm the diagnosis. By working together, healthcare providers can ensure that patients receive the most appropriate and effective care for their condition.

For patients, understanding a diagnosis can be a complex and emotional process. It is essential for patients to educate themselves about their condition, ask questions, and seek support from healthcare providers, family members, and other resources. Patients may also benefit from joining patient support groups or seeking counseling to cope with the emotional impact of a diagnosis. By taking an active role in their care and seeking information and support, patients can better manage their condition and make informed decisions about treatment. By working together to explain the diagnosis, explore treatment options, and address the patient's concerns and preferences, healthcare providers can empower patients to take control of their health and well-being. Patients, in turn, can educate themselves about their condition, seek support, and participate in their care to achieve the best possible outcomes. With open communication, collaboration, and support, patients and healthcare providers can navigate the challenges of a diagnosis and work together towards optimal health and quality of life.

Chapter 3: Treatment options for ADHD

- MEDICATION

Medication plays a crucial role in the field of healthcare, as it is a primary method of treating and managing various medical conditions. Medications are substances used to diagnose, treat, cure, or prevent disease. They can be found in various forms such as pills, tablets, syrups, creams, injections, and patches. Medications work by entering the body and interacting with its cells and tissues to produce a desired effect. They can help alleviate symptoms, control chronic conditions, or even save lives in emergencies.

One of the key components of medication is the active ingredient, which is the chemical substance responsible for the medication's therapeutic effects. Active ingredients are carefully selected based on their ability to target specific biochemical pathways or processes in the body. For example, pain medications such as ibuprofen work by inhibiting the production of prostaglandins, which are chemicals that cause inflammation and pain. By understanding how medications interact with the body at a molecular level, healthcare providers can tailor treatment plans to individual patients and optimize therapeutic outcomes.

It is essential to use medications responsibly and according to healthcare provider instructions. This includes taking medications at the prescribed dosage and frequency, as well as following any dietary or lifestyle recommendations that may be necessary for the medication to work effectively. Failure to adhere to medication instructions can lead to adverse effects, drug interactions, or treatment failure. It is also important to be aware of potential side effects or allergic reactions that may occur while taking medication. If any adverse reactions are experienced, it is crucial to consult with a healthcare provider immediately.

In addition to prescribed medications, over-the-counter (OTC) medications are also widely available for self-treatment of common ailments. OTC medications can provide relief for symptoms such as headaches, allergies, colds, and minor aches and pains. While OTC medications are generally safe for most people to use, it is important to read and follow the instructions on the label carefully. Some OTC medications may interact with prescription medications or have contraindications for certain medical conditions. Consulting with a pharmacist or healthcare provider before starting any new OTC medication is recommended, especially for individuals with pre-existing health conditions or who are taking multiple medications.

The field of pharmacology encompasses the study of how medications work in the body, including their mechanisms of action, pharmacokinetics (how the body processes medications), pharmacodynamics (how medications interact with their targets), and toxicity profiles. Pharmacologists play a critical role in drug development, evaluating the safety and efficacy of new medications through preclinical and clinical trials. By understanding the pharmacological properties of medications, healthcare providers can make informed decisions about drug therapy and monitor patients for potential side effects or drug interactions.

Pharmacists are healthcare professionals who specialize in medication management and dispensing. Pharmacists play a vital role in ensuring the safe and effective use of medications by counseling patients on proper medication use, monitoring for potential drug interactions, and collaborating with healthcare providers to optimize treatment outcomes. Pharmacists also play a key role in medication safety initiatives, such as medication reconciliation programs to prevent medication errors during transitions of care. By leveraging their knowledge of pharmacology, pharmacists can help patients achieve better health outcomes through personalized medication management strategies. Understanding the mechanisms of action, pharmacological properties, and safe use of medications is critical for healthcare providers and patients alike. By working collaboratively with healthcare providers, pharmacists, and other members of the healthcare team, patients can optimize their medication therapy and achieve optimal health outcomes. Through responsible medication use, adherence to treatment plans, and ongoing monitoring for potential side effects, individuals can benefit from the therapeutic effects of medications while minimizing the risks associated with drug therapy.

- Therapy

Therapy is a broad and versatile field that encompasses a wide range of approaches to help individuals address their mental health concerns and improve overall well-being. From traditional psychotherapy to more specialized techniques such as cognitive-behavioral therapy and dialectical behavior therapy, there is a therapy modality to suit the unique needs and preferences of each individual. The ultimate goal of therapy is to provide a safe and supportive environment for clients to explore their thoughts, feelings, and behaviors, identify patterns that may be contributing to their distress, and develop coping strategies to navigate life's challenges more effectively.

One of the key principles that underlies all forms of therapy is the belief in the power of the therapeutic relationship. Research has consistently shown that the quality of the bond between therapist and client is one of the strongest predictors of therapeutic success. A warm, empathetic, and nonjudgmental therapist can create a space where clients feel heard, validated, and understood, which in turn can help them open up and explore their inner world more deeply. This trusting relationship provides a foundation for the therapeutic work to unfold, allowing clients to explore difficult emotions, confront challenging beliefs, and learn new ways of relating to themselves and others.

Therapy is not a one-size-fits-all solution, and different modalities may be more effective for different individuals and concerns. For example, cognitive-behavioral therapy (CBT) is a structured, goal-oriented approach that focuses on changing unhelpful thought patterns and behaviors to improve mood and reduce symptoms of anxiety and depression. Dialectical behavior therapy (DBT), on the other hand, is a skills-based approach that focuses on increasing emotional regulation, distress tolerance, and interpersonal effectiveness. Each of these modalities has its own strengths and limitations, and a skilled therapist will work collaboratively with clients to determine the best approach based on their unique needs and goals.

In addition to individual therapy, group therapy and family therapy can also be valuable tools for addressing mental health concerns. Group therapy provides a supportive environment for individuals to connect with others who may be facing similar challenges, share experiences, and learn new coping skills. Family therapy, on the other hand, focuses on improving communication and relationships within the family system, addressing underlying patterns of conflict and dysfunction that may be contributing to individual distress. These modalities can be particularly effective for addressing issues such as addiction, trauma, and relationship conflicts, where the involvement of multiple individuals can play a key role in the healing process.

It is important to recognize that therapy is not a quick fix or a cure-all for mental health concerns. It is a collaborative process that requires time, effort, and commitment from both the client and the therapist. Just as physical health requires ongoing care and maintenance, mental health also requires regular attention and support to thrive. Therapy can provide a safe space for individuals to explore their inner world, confront difficult emotions, and learn new coping skills, but ultimately it is up to the individual to apply these insights and strategies to their daily life. With dedication and perseverance, therapy can be a powerful tool for personal growth, healing, and transformation.

- Behavior management techniques

Behavior management techniques are essential tools for educators, therapists, and parents to effectively address challenging behaviors in children and individuals with developmental disabilities. These techniques are grounded in principles of behavior analysis, which emphasize the role of environmental factors in shaping and maintaining behaviors. By understanding the functions of behavior and implementing evidence-based strategies, professionals can help individuals learn new, adaptive behaviors and decrease problematic behaviors.

One key aspect of behavior management techniques is the use of positive reinforcement. Positive reinforcement involves providing rewards or consequences that increase the likelihood of a behavior occurring again in the future. This can be as simple as giving praise or a sticker for completing a task, or offering a preferred activity as a reward for good behavior. By consistently reinforcing desired behaviors, individuals are more motivated to continue engaging in those behaviors. Positive reinforcement is particularly effective when applied immediately after the desired behavior occurs, as it helps to strengthen the association between the behavior and the reward.

Another important behavior management technique is the use of functional behavior assessment (FBA) to identify the underlying reasons for problematic behaviors. FBA involves looking at the antecedents (triggers) and consequences of a behavior to determine what is causing it to occur. By understanding the function of a behavior, professionals can develop targeted intervention strategies that address the root cause of the behavior. For example, if a child is engaging in tantrum behavior to escape a difficult task, the key is to find ways to make the task more manageable or rewarding for the child to reduce the need for escape-maintained behaviors.

In addition to positive reinforcement and functional behavior assessment, behavior management techniques also include strategies for implementing consequences for challenging behaviors. Consequences can be both positive and negative, depending on the context and the function of the behavior. For example, if a child engages in aggressive behavior towards peers, a consequence may involve a time-out or loss of privileges. It is important for consequences to be consistent, fair, and appropriate for the behavior in question. When consequences are applied in a timely and consistent manner, individuals are more likely to learn from their actions and make better choices in the future.

Behavior management techniques also include strategies for teaching and reinforcing alternative behaviors. Instead of focusing solely on decreasing problematic behaviors, professionals should also emphasize teaching individuals new, adaptive behaviors to replace the ones that are causing difficulties. This can involve breaking down complex skills into smaller, more manageable steps, providing clear instructions and guidance, and offering plenty of opportunities for practice and reinforcement. By teaching individuals alternative behaviors that serve the same function as the problematic behavior, professionals can help individuals build a repertoire of skills that promote success and independence. By understanding the principles of behavior analysis, implementing positive reinforcement, conducting functional behavior assessments, applying consequences effectively, and teaching alternative behaviors, professionals can help individuals learn new skills, reduce problem behaviors, and improve their overall quality of life. By using evidence-based strategies and individualized interventions, professionals can make a positive impact on the lives of those they work with and empower them to reach their full potential.

Chapter 4: Creating a supportive home environment

- ESTABLISHING ROUTINES

Establishing routines is an essential aspect of daily life that helps individuals maintain structure, discipline, and productivity. Routines can encompass a wide range of activities, from basic daily tasks such as waking up and eating meals to more complex processes like studying or exercising.

One of the key benefits of establishing routines is the ability to streamline daily tasks and make them more efficient. By setting specific times for activities such as waking up, eating meals, and working out, individuals can create a sense of order in their day and ensure that they are making the most of their time. This can help to reduce decision fatigue and make it easier to prioritize tasks effectively. Additionally, routines can help individuals build healthy habits by creating consistency in their behavior, which can lead to long-term positive changes in their lifestyle.

Furthermore, routines can help individuals develop a sense of discipline and self-control. By committing to a schedule and sticking to it every day, individuals can build resilience and determination to overcome challenges and achieve their goals. This can be particularly beneficial in areas such as work, school, or fitness, where consistency and dedication are key to success. By establishing routines, individuals can develop a strong sense of accountability and responsibility, which can help them stay focused and motivated in pursuing their objectives.

In addition to promoting efficiency and discipline, routines can also have a positive impact on mental health and well-being. By creating a sense of structure and predictability in their lives, individuals can reduce feelings of anxiety and uncertainty. Routines can provide a sense of stability and security, which can help individuals feel more in control of their circumstances. This can be particularly beneficial during times of stress or change, as routines can serve as a source of comfort and reassurance.

When it comes to establishing routines, there are several strategies that individuals can use to set themselves up for success. One of the most important steps is to identify key activities that are important to incorporate into a daily routine. This can include tasks such as exercise, meal prep, work, study, and self-care. By prioritizing these activities and allocating specific time slots for them in a schedule, individuals can ensure that they are dedicating enough time and energy to each task. Additionally, it can be helpful to set specific goals and deadlines for each activity to keep oneself accountable and motivated.

Another important aspect of establishing routines is to create a consistent daily schedule. This can involve setting specific wake-up and bedtime routines, meal times, work or study hours, and relaxation periods. By following a consistent schedule, individuals can train their bodies and minds to expect certain activities at certain times, which can help to establish a sense of rhythm and flow in their day. It is also important to be flexible and adaptable with routines, as unexpected events or changes may require adjustments to be made. By being open to making changes when necessary, individuals can maintain a sense of control and balance in their routines. By setting specific times for activities, individuals can streamline their tasks and make the most of their time. Routines can also help individuals develop discipline and self-control, leading to increased productivity and success. Additionally, routines can have a positive impact on mental health and well-being by providing a sense of stability and predictability. By following strategies such as identifying key activities, creating a consistent schedule, and being flexible when necessary, individuals can establish routines that contribute to a healthy and balanced lifestyle.

- Setting clear expectations

Setting clear expectations is a critical aspect of effective communication in any professional or academic setting. By clearly outlining what is expected of individuals, teams, or organizations, clarity and focus can be achieved to ensure successful outcomes. When expectations are not clearly defined, misunderstandings, confusion, and potential conflicts can arise, leading to inefficiencies and poor performance. By setting clear expectations, everyone involved can have a clear understanding of their roles, responsibilities, and goals, which can help foster collaboration and productivity.

One key element of setting clear expectations is defining specific and measurable objectives. By clearly outlining what needs to be achieved and how success will be measured, individuals can have a clear roadmap for their efforts. This can help to ensure that everyone is working towards the same goal and can track progress effectively. For example, in a team project, setting clear objectives for each team member can help ensure that everyone is contributing their fair share and that progress is being made towards the overall goal. By setting specific and measurable objectives, individuals can have a clear understanding of what is expected of them and can adjust their efforts accordingly.

In addition to defining specific objectives, setting clear expectations also involves outlining the necessary resources and support needed to achieve those objectives. This can include providing access to tools, training, and information that individuals may need to successfully complete their tasks. By clearly communicating what resources are available and how they can be accessed, individuals can feel supported and empowered to achieve their goals. For example, in an academic setting, providing students with access to research materials, study resources, and academic support services can help ensure that they have what they need to succeed in their coursework.

Furthermore, setting clear expectations also involves defining timelines and deadlines for completion. By establishing clear deadlines for tasks and projects, individuals can prioritize their efforts and work efficiently towards achieving their goals. This can help prevent procrastination and ensure that progress is being made in a timely manner. For example, in a professional setting, setting deadlines for project milestones can help keep teams on track and ensure that projects are completed on time. By clearly communicating deadlines and expectations for completion, individuals can plan their work effectively and avoid last-minute rushes to meet objectives.

Another important aspect of setting clear expectations is providing feedback and guidance along the way. By regularly checking in with individuals to provide feedback on their progress and offering guidance on how to improve, expectations can be managed effectively. This can help individuals identify areas where they may need additional support or resources, and can also help to celebrate successes and progress towards goals. For example, in a professional setting, regular performance reviews can help employees understand how they are meeting expectations and where there may be room for improvement. By providing constructive feedback and guidance, individuals can feel supported and motivated to continue working towards their goals. By defining specific objectives, providing necessary resources and support, establishing timelines and deadlines, and offering feedback and guidance, individuals can have a clear understanding of what is expected of them and how to succeed. By setting clear expectations, organizations can create a positive and productive work environment where everyone can work towards shared goals and achieve success.

- Managing distractions

In today's fast-paced world, distractions are everywhere. From notifications popping up on our smartphones to the constant stream of emails flooding our inboxes, it can be challenging to stay focused on the task at hand. However, managing distractions is crucial for productivity and overall well-being. In this essay, we will explore the importance of managing distractions, techniques for minimizing their impact, and strategies for maintaining focus in an increasingly distracting environment.

Distractions can come in many forms, both external and internal. External distractions include noise, interruptions from colleagues, and technology such as social media and emails. Internal distractions, on the other hand, can stem from our own thoughts and emotions, such as anxiety, boredom, or lack of motivation. Regardless of their origin, distractions can derail our efforts to complete tasks efficiently and effectively.

One of the main reasons why managing distractions is so important is that they can have a significant impact on our productivity. When we are constantly interrupted or pulled away from our work, it can take time to refocus and get back into a state of flow. This not only slows us down but also reduces the quality of our work. In fact, research has shown that even brief distractions can lead to a decrease in cognitive performance and an increase in errors.

Therefore, by learning how to manage distractions, we can improve our ability to concentrate and produce high-quality work.

In addition to affecting our productivity, distractions can also have a negative impact on our well-being. When we are constantly bombarded with stimuli, it can be difficult to relax and unwind, leading to feelings of stress and overwhelm. Furthermore, constantly switching between tasks can increase our levels of cortisol, a stress hormone that can have detrimental effects on our physical and mental health. By managing distractions and creating a more focused work environment, we can reduce our stress levels and improve our overall well-being.

So, how can we effectively manage distractions in our daily lives. One key strategy is to create a distraction-free environment. This may involve setting boundaries with colleagues, turning off notifications on our devices, or working in a quiet, dedicated space. By eliminating potential distractions before they have a chance to disrupt our work, we can create a more conducive environment for concentration and focus.

Another important technique for managing distractions is to practice mindfulness. By paying attention to our thoughts and emotions in the present moment, we can become more aware of when distractions arise and take steps to address them. This may involve taking deep breaths, practicing meditation, or simply reminding ourselves to stay focused on the task at hand. By cultivating a sense of mindfulness, we can improve our ability to resist distractions and maintain our concentration for longer periods of time.

In addition to creating a distraction-free environment and practicing mindfulness, it can also be helpful to establish a routine or schedule for our work. By setting aside dedicated time for focused work and breaking tasks into smaller, manageable chunks, we can reduce the likelihood of becoming overwhelmed and distracted. This can also help us prioritize our tasks and stay on track, ensuring that we are making progress towards our goals.

To bring to a close, it can be beneficial to consciously limit our exposure to distractions, especially those that are particularly difficult to resist (e. g. , social media). This may involve setting strict boundaries for when and how we use these technologies, or even temporarily disconnecting from them altogether. By taking control of our environment and reducing the temptation of distractions, we can increase our ability to focus and achieve our desired outcomes. By understanding the impact of distractions on our productivity and well-being, and implementing strategies for minimizing their influence, we can create a more focused and effective work environment. By creating a distraction-free environment, practicing mindfulness, establishing a routine, and limiting exposure to distractions, we can enhance our ability to concentrate, produce high-quality work, and ultimately achieve our goals.

Chapter 5: Communicating effectively with your child

- ACTIVE LISTENING SKILLS

Active listening skills are essential in various contexts, including professional settings, academic environments, and personal relationships. This communication technique involves fully concentrating on what the speaker is saying, understanding their message, responding appropriately, and providing feedback to ensure mutual understanding. By actively engaging in the listening process, individuals can demonstrate empathy, build trust, and strengthen their relationships with others.

To develop active listening skills, one must first understand the importance of being fully present and mentally focused during conversations. This means setting aside distractions, such as cell phones or other electronic devices, and giving the speaker your undivided attention. By making eye contact, nodding in agreement, and using verbal cues to show that you are listening, you can convey your interest and attentiveness to the speaker. This not only fosters a sense of respect and appreciation but also encourages the speaker to continue sharing their thoughts and feelings.

In addition to being physically present, active listening requires individuals to engage in the process of decoding and interpreting the speaker's message. This involves paying attention to not only what is being said but also how it is being said, including the speaker's tone of voice, body language, and facial expressions. By analyzing these nonverbal cues, listeners can gain a deeper understanding of the speaker's emotions, intentions, and underlying message.

This allows for more effective communication and helps to prevent misunderstandings or misinterpretations.

Furthermore, active listening involves responding and providing feedback to the speaker to demonstrate understanding and promote dialogue. This can be done by paraphrasing the speaker's words, asking clarifying questions, or reflecting back what was said to ensure accuracy. By actively engaging in the conversation and showing that you are actively listening, you can create an open and respectful communication environment where all parties feel heard and valued. This not only fosters mutual understanding but also encourages the speaker to share their thoughts and feelings more openly and honestly.

Moreover, active listening skills are crucial in professional settings as they can enhance collaboration, problem-solving, and decision-making processes. By actively listening to colleagues, clients, or stakeholders, individuals can gain valuable insights, perspectives, and feedback that can inform their work and help them make more informed decisions. Active listening also promotes a culture of respect, trust, and empathy in the workplace, which can improve team dynamics, productivity, and overall job satisfaction. By honing their active listening skills, professionals can build stronger relationships, resolve conflicts more effectively, and achieve greater success in their careers.

In academic environments, active listening skills are equally important as they can enhance learning, critical thinking, and communication abilities. By actively listening to instructors, classmates, or peers, students can gain a deeper understanding of course material, engage in meaningful discussions, and develop their analytical and problem-solving skills. Active listening also fosters a sense of respect, empathy, and collaboration in academic settings, which can lead to more productive group projects, research initiatives, and academic achievements. By practicing active listening, students can improve their academic performance, develop stronger relationships with their peers and instructors, and enhance their overall learning experience. By developing the ability to listen actively and attentively, individuals can enhance their listening comprehension, empathy, and overall communication effectiveness. Whether in professional settings, academic environments, or personal relationships, active listening can foster mutual understanding, trust, and respect, which are critical components of successful communication. By honing their active listening skills, individuals can improve their relationships, enhance their problem-solving abilities, and achieve greater success in their professional and personal lives.

- Encouraging open dialogue

Open dialogue refers to the exchange of thoughts, ideas, and opinions between individuals or groups in a manner that is respectful, constructive, and conducive to mutual understanding. It is an essential component of effective communication, as it allows for the free flow of information and the exchange of perspectives. Encouraging open dialogue fosters collaboration, creativity, and innovation, as it enables individuals to share their thoughts and ideas without fear of judgment or reprisal.

One of the key benefits of open dialogue is that it promotes a culture of transparency and trust within an organization or community. When individuals feel comfortable expressing their thoughts and opinions openly, they are more likely to feel valued and respected by their peers and colleagues. This, in turn, can lead to increased morale, productivity, and job satisfaction, as employees feel empowered to contribute their ideas and suggestions to the group. Additionally, open dialogue can help to identify and address potential issues or conflicts at an early stage, before they escalate into more serious problems.

Encouraging open dialogue also helps to break down barriers and build bridges between individuals from different backgrounds or perspectives. By creating opportunities for people to share their experiences, values, and beliefs, open dialogue can promote empathy, understanding, and tolerance among diverse groups. This can be particularly important in today's globalized and multicultural society, where people from different cultures, religions, and social backgrounds often come into contact with one another. By engaging in open dialogue, individuals can learn to appreciate and respect the perspectives of others, even if they may not always agree with them.

In addition to fostering a culture of transparency and understanding, open dialogue can also stimulate creativity and innovation within an organization or community. When individuals have the freedom to express their thoughts and ideas freely, they are more likely to come up with new and innovative solutions to problems or challenges. By encouraging open dialogue, organizations can tap into the collective wisdom and creativity of their employees, leading to more effective and sustainable outcomes. Moreover, open dialogue can also help to identify and address potential blind spots or biases within an organization, by allowing individuals to challenge conventional wisdom and explore new ways of thinking.

While the benefits of open dialogue are clear, it is important to recognize that creating and maintaining an environment that encourages open dialogue can be challenging. Individuals may feel hesitant to express their thoughts or opinions freely, for fear of judgment, ridicule, or backlash from others. Moreover, entrenched power dynamics, hierarchical structures, and cultural norms within an organization or community can also inhibit open dialogue and stifle diverse perspectives. In order to overcome these obstacles, it is important for leaders to create a safe and inclusive environment where individuals feel empowered to speak up and contribute their ideas.

One effective way to encourage open dialogue is to model the behavior yourself as a leader. By demonstrating good listening skills, empathy, and respect for others' opinions, you can set a positive example for your team or organization. Encourage and reward open communication by actively seeking out and valuing input from all members of your team, regardless of their seniority or position. Create opportunities for open dialogue through regular team meetings, brainstorming sessions, or informal discussions, where individuals can share their thoughts and ideas freely. Provide training and support to help individuals develop their communication skills and confidence in expressing their opinions. And most importantly, be open to feedback and criticism yourself, and be willing to engage in constructive dialogue with others, even if it means challenging your own assumptions or beliefs. By fostering a culture of respect, empathy, and understanding, leaders can create a safe and inclusive environment where individuals feel empowered to share their thoughts and ideas freely. Through open dialogue, organizations can tap into the collective wisdom and creativity of their employees, leading to more effective and sustainable outcomes. By embracing open dialogue as a core value, leaders can help to build stronger connections, foster collaboration, and drive positive change within their organizations and communities.

- Using positive reinforcement

Positive reinforcement is a powerful tool that can be used to shape behavior and promote learning in a wide variety of settings, including classrooms, workplaces, and even homes. By using positive reinforcement techniques, individuals can be encouraged to engage in desired behaviors through the use of rewards or praise. This approach is based on the principles of operant conditioning, a psychological theory developed by B. F. Skinner in the mid-20th century.

One of the key advantages of using positive reinforcement is that it can help to create a supportive and motivating environment for individuals. By providing positive feedback and rewards for desired behaviors, individuals are more likely to repeat those behaviors in the future. This can lead to increased motivation, improved performance, and a greater sense of accomplishment. In contrast to punishment-based techniques, which can be demotivating and may lead to negative emotional reactions, positive reinforcement focuses on rewarding and encouraging positive behavior.

Another benefit of positive reinforcement is that it can help to build positive relationships and nurture a sense of trust and respect between individuals. When positive reinforcement is used consistently and effectively, individuals are more likely to feel valued and appreciated, leading to improved communication and collaboration. This can be particularly important in educational settings, where positive teacher-student relationships have been shown to be associated with higher levels of student engagement and academic achievement. By using positive reinforcement, educators can create a supportive and inclusive learning environment where all students have the opportunity to succeed.

Positive reinforcement can also be an effective tool for promoting social and emotional development. By recognizing and rewarding positive behaviors such as kindness, empathy, and cooperation, individuals can learn important social skills and emotional intelligence. This can help to foster a sense of empathy and understanding towards others, as well as develop important life skills such as problem-solving and conflict resolution. In addition, positive reinforcement can help individuals to build self-esteem and self-confidence, as they receive positive feedback and recognition for their efforts.

It is important to note that positive reinforcement should be used in a thoughtful and strategic manner to be effective. In order to maximize the benefits of positive reinforcement, it is important to clearly define the desired behaviors and establish clear and consistent rewards or reinforcements. It is also important to consider individual differences and tailor the approach to meet the needs of each individual or group. By taking the time to assess the specific goals and needs of the situation, positive reinforcement can be used to effectively promote positive behavior and support learning and growth. By providing rewards and recognition for desired behaviors, individuals can be motivated to engage in positive actions and habits. Positive reinforcement can help to create a supportive and motivating environment, build positive relationships, promote social and emotional development, and foster a sense of self-esteem and self-confidence. By using positive reinforcement in a thoughtful and strategic manner, individuals can be empowered to reach their full potential and achieve success in their personal and professional lives.

Chapter 6: Building a strong support network

- INVOLVING TEACHERS and caregivers

Involving teachers and caregivers in the education and development of children is crucial for their overall well-being and success. Teachers play a significant role in shaping the academic and social skills of children, while caregivers provide important support and guidance outside of the classroom. By working together, teachers and caregivers can create a cohesive and supportive environment that fosters the growth and development of children.

One of the key benefits of involving teachers and caregivers in a child's education is the continuity of care and instruction. Teachers and caregivers can communicate regularly to ensure that they are both working towards the same goals and objectives for the child. This collaboration can help to create a seamless transition between home and school, providing the child with consistency and stability in their learning environment. This continuity can have a positive impact on a child's academic performance and overall well-being.

Furthermore, involving teachers and caregivers in a child's education can lead to a more holistic approach to their development. Teachers and caregivers bring different perspectives and experiences to the table, which can enrich the child's learning experience. Caregivers, for example, may have unique insights into the child's interests, strengths, and challenges that can help teachers tailor their instruction to better meet the child's needs. By working together, teachers and caregivers can create a comprehensive support system that addresses all aspects of a child's development.

In addition to providing continuity and a holistic approach to education, involving teachers and caregivers can also help to build a strong support network for the child. Teachers and caregivers can share resources, strategies, and best practices to ensure the child receives the best possible care and education. This collaborative support network can be particularly beneficial for children who may have special needs or require additional support. By working together, teachers and caregivers can create a customized plan that meets the unique needs of the child and helps them thrive academically and socially.

Another important benefit of involving teachers and caregivers in a child's education is the reinforcement of positive behaviors and values. Children learn by example, and when teachers and caregivers model positive behaviors and values, they are more likely to be internalized by the child. By working together to promote a set of shared values and expectations, teachers and caregivers can create a consistent and supportive environment that reinforces positive behavior and promotes the development of important life skills such as empathy, responsibility, and resilience. By working together, teachers and caregivers can provide continuity, a holistic approach to education, a strong support network, and reinforcement of positive behaviors and values. By collaborating and communicating effectively, teachers and caregivers can create a cohesive and supportive environment that fosters the growth and development of children. It is important for teachers and caregivers to recognize the valuable role they play in shaping the future of the next generation and to work together to ensure that every child has the opportunity to reach their full potential.

- Joining support groups

Support groups are an invaluable resource for individuals seeking to connect with others who share similar experiences and challenges. By joining a support group, individuals can find a sense of community, understanding, and validation that can be difficult to find elsewhere. Support groups offer a safe space for members to share their feelings, fears, and struggles without fear of judgment or stigma. This sense of solidarity can be incredibly empowering and can help individuals feel less alone in their struggles.

One of the key benefits of joining a support group is the opportunity to gain valuable insights and perspectives from others who have navigated similar challenges. By sharing their experiences, members can learn from one another and gain new strategies for coping with their own difficulties. This exchange of knowledge and support can be a powerful tool for personal growth and healing. Additionally, support groups provide a platform for members to offer and receive encouragement and motivation, which can be incredibly uplifting and empowering.

Support groups also offer a sense of accountability and structure that can be beneficial for individuals who are struggling to cope with their challenges on their own. By regularly attending group meetings and engaging with other members, individuals can stay motivated and committed to their own personal growth and healing. Support groups can also provide a sense of belonging and acceptance that can be incredibly healing for individuals who may feel isolated or alone in their struggles.

In addition to the emotional support and camaraderie that support groups offer, they can also provide practical guidance and resources for individuals seeking to overcome their challenges. Support groups often have access to valuable information, tools, and professional guidance that can help members navigate their difficulties more effectively. This can include information about therapy options, self-care practices, and coping strategies that have been proven to be effective for others in similar situations. By tapping into the collective wisdom of the group, members can gain a deeper understanding of their challenges and the tools they need to navigate them successfully.

Support groups can also be an important source of validation and affirmation for individuals who may be struggling with feelings of shame or self-doubt. By connecting with others who have experienced similar challenges, individuals can gain a sense of perspective and understanding that can help them shift their own self-perception. This validation can be incredibly empowering and can help individuals feel more confident in their ability to navigate their challenges and overcome their difficulties. In this way, support groups can play a crucial role in fostering self-acceptance and self-compassion, which are essential ingredients for personal growth and healing. By providing a safe space for members to share their feelings, experiences, and insights, support groups offer a powerful platform for growth, healing, and connection. Support groups provide emotional support, practical guidance, and validation that can be invaluable for individuals who may be struggling to cope with their challenges on their own. By tapping into the collective wisdom, support, and resources of the group, members can gain new perspectives, tools, and strategies for navigating their difficulties more effectively. Ultimately, support groups offer a sense of community, understanding, and empowerment that can help individuals feel less alone in their struggles and more confident in their ability to overcome their challenges.

- Accessing community resources

Accessing community resources is a crucial aspect of fostering a healthy and thriving community. Community resources encompass a wide range of services, programs, and facilities that are available to residents to support their well-being and enhance their quality of life. These resources can include community centers, libraries, healthcare services, social services, job training programs, recreational facilities, and much more. Accessing these resources can greatly benefit individuals and families by providing them with the support they need to navigate life's challenges and achieve their goals.

One of the key benefits of accessing community resources is the opportunity to connect with others in the community. Community resources often provide a space for residents to come together, socialize, and build relationships with their neighbors. This sense of community connection can help reduce feelings of isolation and loneliness, improve mental health, and increase overall well-being. By participating in community programs and activities, individuals can expand their social networks, cultivate new friendships, and feel more engaged and connected to the community as a whole.

In addition to fostering social connections, accessing community resources can also provide individuals with valuable support and assistance. Many community resources offer services and programs designed to help residents address specific needs or challenges they may be facing. For example, community health clinics provide affordable healthcare services to uninsured or underinsured individuals, while job training programs offer opportunities for residents to develop new skills and advance their careers. By accessing these resources, individuals can receive the support they need to overcome obstacles and achieve their personal and professional goals.

Furthermore, accessing community resources can play a vital role in promoting equity and inclusion within a community. By making resources and services readily available to all residents, regardless of their background or circumstances, communities can help ensure that everyone has access to the support they need to thrive. This can help reduce disparities in access to essential services and opportunities, and create a more equitable and inclusive community for all. By actively engaging with community resources and advocating for the needs of marginalized populations, individuals can contribute to building a more just and equitable society for everyone.

When it comes to accessing community resources, there are a few key steps that individuals can take to make the process easier and more effective. First and foremost, it's important to familiarize oneself with the range of resources available in the community. This can involve researching online, speaking with neighbors or community leaders, or visiting local community centers or libraries to learn about the services and programs that are offered. By gaining a better understanding of the available resources, individuals can better identify the ones that are most relevant to their needs and interests.

Once individuals have identified the community resources that they would like to access, the next step is to determine how to access them. Many community resources have specific eligibility requirements or application processes that individuals must follow in order to access services. This can involve completing an application form, attending an orientation session, or meeting with a staff member for an initial assessment. By closely following the guidelines and requirements set forth by the resource provider, individuals can increase their chances of successfully accessing the services they need.

In some cases, individuals may encounter barriers or challenges when trying to access community resources. These barriers can include limited availability of services, eligibility restrictions, language barriers, or lack of transportation. In order to overcome these barriers, individuals can explore alternative options, seek support from community organizations or social services agencies, or advocate for changes to improve access to resources for all residents. By actively addressing barriers to access and working together to create a more inclusive and accessible community, individuals can help ensure that everyone has the opportunity to benefit from the resources available in their community. By connecting with others, seeking support, promoting equity and inclusion, and actively engaging with the resources available, individuals can enhance their quality of life, build meaningful relationships, and contribute to the well-being of the community as a whole. By taking proactive steps to identify and access community resources, individuals can empower themselves to overcome challenges, achieve their goals, and create a more supportive and thriving community for everyone.

Chapter 7: Helping your child succeed in school

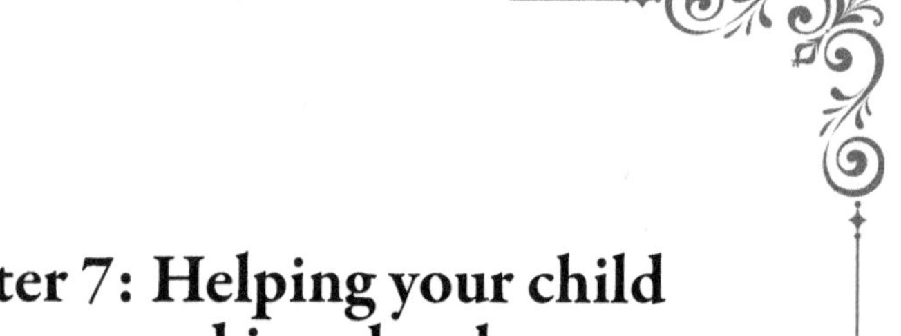

- ACCOMMODATIONS AND modifications

Accommodations and modifications are important tools in the field of education that aim to provide individualized support to students with diverse learning needs. These strategies are designed to help students access the curriculum, participate in classroom activities, and demonstrate their knowledge and skills in a way that is fair and equitable. While accommodations are changes to the environment, instruction, or materials that make it easier for students to learn, modifications involve altering the content or performance expectations to better suit the student's abilities and needs.

One key aspect of accommodations and modifications is the concept of Universal Design for Learning (UDL), which emphasizes the importance of creating inclusive and accessible learning environments for all students. By incorporating UDL principles into instruction, educators can proactively address the diverse needs of students and provide multiple means of engagement, representation, and expression. This approach helps to minimize barriers to learning and ensures that all students have the opportunity to succeed.

Accommodations and modifications can take many forms and may vary depending on the individual needs of the student. Examples of accommodations include providing extra time for assignments or assessments, offering preferential seating, providing visual aids or assistive technology, or allowing breaks during lessons. Modifications, on the other hand, may involve simplifying the content, adjusting the difficulty level of assignments, or providing alternative assessment methods.

It is important for educators to collaborate with students, parents, and other professionals to determine the most appropriate accommodations and modifications for each student. This collaborative approach ensures that the strategies implemented are tailored to the student's unique strengths, challenges, and learning style. By working together, educators can gather valuable insights into the student's needs and preferences, which can inform the decision-making process and lead to more effective support.

In addition to collaborating with stakeholders, educators can benefit from training and professional development on accommodations and modifications. By enhancing their knowledge and skills in this area, educators can better meet the diverse needs of their students and create more inclusive and supportive learning environments. Professional development opportunities may include workshops, seminars, conferences, or online courses that focus on understanding the principles of UDL, implementing effective accommodations and modifications, and evaluating the impact of these strategies on student learning.

Monitoring and evaluating the effectiveness of accommodations and modifications is essential for ensuring that students are making progress and achieving their academic goals. Educators can use a variety of tools and strategies, such as ongoing assessment, progress monitoring, and feedback from students and parents, to gauge the impact of the accommodations and modifications being used. By regularly reviewing and adjusting these strategies based on student feedback and performance data, educators can ensure that students are receiving the support they need to be successful. By implementing a variety of accommodations and modifications, educators can create inclusive and accessible learning environments that support the success of all students. By collaborating with stakeholders, seeking professional development opportunities, and monitoring the effectiveness of these strategies, educators can ensure that students are receiving the individualized support they need to reach their full potential.

- Advocating for your child

Advocating for your child is a crucial aspect of parenting that involves speaking up on behalf of your child's needs, rights, and best interests. As a parent, it is your responsibility to ensure that your child receives the support and resources they require to thrive both academically and socially. This may involve advocating for accommodations or modifications in school settings, seeking out appropriate healthcare services, or addressing any other challenges your child may face. Advocating for your child requires a proactive and assertive approach, as well as effective communication with teachers, healthcare providers, and other important stakeholders in your child's life.

One key aspect of advocating for your child is understanding and effectively communicating your child's needs. This involves developing a deep understanding of your child's strengths, challenges, and unique learning style. By closely observing your child and seeking input from teachers, therapists, and other professionals, you can gain valuable insights into what supports and accommodations are necessary to help your child succeed. By articulating these needs clearly and confidently, you can ensure that your child receives the appropriate services and resources they require to reach their full potential.

In addition to understanding your child's needs, advocating for your child also involves being knowledgeable about your rights and the resources available to you and your child. Familiarize yourself with relevant laws and regulations, such as the Individuals with Disabilities Education Act (IDEA) and Section 504 of the Rehabilitation Act, which protect the rights of children with disabilities and ensure access to appropriate educational services. By knowing your rights and advocating for your child within the framework of these laws, you can effectively navigate the educational system, healthcare system, and other support systems to ensure that your child receives the services and accommodations they require.

Effective advocacy for your child also requires building strong partnerships with key stakeholders, such as teachers, healthcare providers, and school administrators. By establishing open lines of communication and working collaboratively with these individuals, you can ensure that your child's needs are understood and addressed in a timely and appropriate manner. Keep in regular contact with your child's teachers and therapists, attend meetings and conferences to discuss your child's progress and any challenges they may be facing, and advocate for appropriate services and supports as needed. By fostering positive and constructive relationships with these important stakeholders, you can create a supportive network that works together to support your child's well-being and success.

It is important to remember that advocating for your child is an ongoing and evolving process. As your child grows and develops, their needs and challenges may change, requiring you to reassess and adjust your advocacy efforts accordingly. Stay informed about your child's progress, seek feedback from teachers and other professionals, and remain proactive in addressing any issues or concerns that arise. By staying vigilant and proactive in advocating for your child, you can ensure that they receive the necessary support and resources to thrive and succeed in all aspects of their life. By advocating for your child effectively and assertively, you can ensure that they receive the support and resources they require to thrive academically, socially, and emotionally. Remember that you are your child's most important advocate, and by speaking up on their behalf, you can help them reach their full potential and lead a fulfilling and successful life.

- Ensuring academic success

Ensuring academic success is a goal that many students aspire to achieve during their educational journey. While the path to academic success may vary from person to person, there are some key strategies that can help students navigate the challenges of academia and reach their full potential. By implementing these strategies, students can improve their academic performance, enhance their learning experience, and ultimately achieve their academic goals.

One of the most important factors in ensuring academic success is effective time management. This involves setting aside dedicated time for studying, completing assignments, and preparing for exams. By creating a schedule and sticking to it, students can avoid procrastination and ensure that they stay on top of their academic responsibilities. Additionally, prioritizing tasks can help students focus on what is most important and allocate their time and energy accordingly.

Another key aspect of academic success is developing good study habits. This includes finding a quiet and organized study space, eliminating distractions, and using effective study techniques. For example, active studying techniques such as summarizing material, creating flashcards, and practicing problem-solving can help students retain information more effectively and improve their understanding of complex concepts. By developing consistent and effective study habits, students can maximize their learning potential and achieve better academic outcomes.

In addition to time management and study habits, seeking help and support when needed is essential for academic success. This includes reaching out to professors, tutors, or classmates for clarification on course material, seeking guidance on assignments or projects, and utilizing academic resources such as writing centers or study groups. By seeking help and actively engaging in the learning process, students can overcome challenges more effectively, deepen their understanding of course material, and ultimately succeed in their academic pursuits.

Furthermore, staying motivated and maintaining a positive attitude can significantly impact academic success. This involves setting realistic goals, celebrating achievements, and staying inspired throughout the learning process. By staying motivated and cultivating a growth mindset, students can overcome setbacks, persevere through challenges, and maintain a sense of enthusiasm and curiosity for learning. Additionally, developing a sense of resilience and perseverance can help students navigate the ups and downs of academia and stay focused on their long-term academic goals. By implementing these strategies and making a commitment to excellence in their academic pursuits, students can enhance their learning experience, improve their academic performance, and achieve their academic goals. Academic success is attainable for all students, regardless of their background or current academic standing, by leveraging the right tools and strategies to overcome challenges and reach their full potential. Through dedication, persistence, and a commitment to personal growth, students can unlock their academic potential and thrive in the educational environment.

Chapter 8: Encouraging positive self-esteem

- BUILDING CONFIDENCE

Confidence is a crucial aspect of our personal and professional development. It allows us to take on challenges, make decisions, and interact with others in a positive and assertive manner. Building confidence is a process that requires self-awareness, practice, and a willingness to step outside of our comfort zones. In this article, we will explore some effective strategies for building confidence and discuss the benefits of doing so.

One of the first steps in building confidence is to identify the areas in which we feel insecure or lacking in self-assurance. This may involve reflecting on past experiences, seeking feedback from others, or engaging in self-assessment exercises. By pinpointing our areas of weakness, we can begin to develop specific strategies for improvement. For example, if we lack confidence in public speaking, we can take a public speaking course, practice speaking in front of a mirror, or join a toastmasters club to hone our skills and build our confidence in this area.

Another key strategy for building confidence is to set achievable goals for ourselves. These goals should be specific, measurable, and time-bound, and should challenge us to step outside of our comfort zones. By setting goals that are both realistic and challenging, we can push ourselves to grow and develop new skills while also building our confidence in the process. For example, if we want to improve our confidence in social situations, we can set a goal of attending a networking event and striking up conversations with at least three new people.

Building confidence also requires us to practice self-compassion and cultivate a positive mindset. This means acknowledging and accepting our imperfections, failures, and setbacks, and learning to treat ourselves with kindness and understanding. By challenging negative self-talk, reframing our beliefs, and focusing on our strengths and accomplishments, we can cultivate a more positive and resilient mindset that will support our confidence-building efforts. It is important to remember that building confidence is a process that takes time and effort, and that setbacks are a natural part of the journey.

In addition to setting goals and cultivating a positive mindset, building confidence also involves taking action and facing our fears head-on. This may involve stepping outside of our comfort zones, trying new things, and practicing skills that we may not feel completely confident in. By taking small, incremental steps towards our goals, we can gradually build our confidence and overcome our fears. For example, if we want to improve our confidence in taking risks, we can start by taking on small challenges, such as speaking up in a meeting or volunteering for a new project, and gradually work our way up to bigger challenges as our confidence grows.

It is also important to seek support and feedback from others as we work to build our confidence. This may involve enlisting the help of a mentor, coach, or therapist who can provide guidance, encouragement, and accountability. It may also involve seeking feedback from colleagues, friends, or family members who can offer constructive criticism and support as we work to improve our confidence. By surrounding ourselves with positive and supportive individuals who believe in our potential, we can strengthen our confidence and build the resilience we need to face challenges and setbacks. By setting achievable goals, cultivating a positive mindset, taking action, and seeking support from others, we can gradually build our confidence and develop the resilience we need to navigate life's challenges with grace and self-assurance. Building confidence is not a one-time event, but an ongoing journey of growth and development that can bring significant benefits to our personal and professional lives. By committing to the process and investing in our own self-belief, we can cultivate the confidence we need to thrive and succeed in all areas of our lives.

- Fostering independence

Fostering independence in individuals is a critical aspect of personal development and growth. It involves empowering individuals to take responsibility for their own actions and decisions, and ultimately become self-reliant and self-sufficient. Independence is not just about autonomy and freedom; it is also about developing the necessary skills, mindset, and attitudes that enable individuals to thrive and succeed in various aspects of life.

One of the key benefits of fostering independence is that it promotes self-confidence and self-esteem. When individuals are given the opportunity to make their own choices and decisions, they learn to trust in their abilities and judgment. This sense of self-confidence and self-belief is essential for personal growth and development, as it enables individuals to overcome challenges and obstacles with resilience and determination.

Independence also fosters a sense of agency and empowerment. When individuals are able to take charge of their own lives and make decisions that align with their values and goals, they feel a greater sense of control and ownership over their circumstances. This empowerment can be incredibly empowering and motivating, as it enables individuals to pursue their aspirations and dreams with a sense of purpose and determination.

Furthermore, fostering independence can lead to increased creativity and innovation. When individuals are empowered to think for themselves and explore new possibilities, they are more likely to come up with unique solutions to problems and challenges. This creativity and innovation can lead to new ideas, inventions, and initiatives that benefit not only the individual but also the wider community and society as a whole.

Independence also cultivates resilience and adaptability. When individuals are accustomed to taking responsibility for their actions and decisions, they are better equipped to cope with setbacks and failures. They are more likely to bounce back from disappointments and setbacks, as they have the confidence and skills to navigate through adversity and emerge stronger and more resilient on the other side.

Moreover, fostering independence can lead to improved relationships and social connections. When individuals are self-reliant and self-sufficient, they are better able to contribute positively to their relationships and communities. They are more likely to communicate effectively, collaborate with others, and offer support and assistance when needed. This can help to build strong, nurturing, and mutually beneficial bonds with others, leading to a sense of belonging and connection. It enables individuals to cultivate self-confidence, agency, creativity, resilience, and social connections, all of which are essential for leading a fulfilling and successful life. By empowering individuals to take responsibility for their own actions and decisions, we can help them to become more capable, resourceful, and empowered individuals who can make a positive impact on the world around them. It is important for educators, parents, and communities to prioritize and support efforts to foster independence in individuals, as it not only benefits the individual but also the wider society as a whole.

- Celebrating achievements

Celebrating achievements is an essential aspect of human life that serves to recognize and commemorate noteworthy accomplishments. Whether it be in the personal, academic, or professional realm, celebrating achievements provides a sense of validation and encouragement for individuals to continue striving towards their goals. It is a way to acknowledge the hard work, dedication, and perseverance that individuals have put into achieving success, and it fosters a sense of pride and satisfaction in one's abilities and capabilities.

In academia, celebrating achievements takes many forms, such as receiving an award, publishing a research paper, or presenting at a conference. These achievements are significant milestones that mark the progress and contributions of individuals in their respective fields. Academic achievements are often the result of years of hard work, research, and dedication, and celebrating them is a way to acknowledge the impact and significance of these accomplishments. Celebrating achievements in academia also serves to inspire and motivate others to pursue their own academic goals and aspirations.

In the professional world, celebrating achievements is a common practice that helps boost morale, foster teamwork, and promote a positive work culture. Recognizing the accomplishments of employees, whether it be meeting a sales target, completing a project ahead of schedule, or securing a new client, is essential for creating a sense of appreciation and recognition in the workplace. By celebrating achievements, employers can demonstrate their appreciation for their employees' hard work and dedication, which can help improve job satisfaction, retention rates, and overall productivity.

On a personal level, celebrating achievements is a way to acknowledge the growth, progress, and accomplishments that individuals have made in their lives. Whether it be reaching a fitness goal, learning a new skill, or overcoming a personal challenge, celebrating achievements provides a sense of satisfaction, pride, and fulfillment. It is a way to recognize one's own worth and abilities, and to celebrate the hard work and dedication that has gone into achieving success. By acknowledging achievements, individuals can feel a sense of validation, pride, and satisfaction in their abilities and capabilities. It is a way to inspire and motivate others to pursue their own goals and aspirations, and to foster a positive work culture and sense of appreciation in the workplace. Celebrating achievements is a powerful tool for recognizing the hard work and dedication that individuals put into achieving success, and it serves to inspire and encourage continued growth and progress.

Chapter 9: Managing behavior challenges

- SETTING BOUNDARIES

Setting boundaries is a crucial aspect of establishing healthy relationships, both in professional and personal spheres. Boundaries are the limits we set for ourselves in terms of what we are willing to accept from others, and what we are comfortable with in terms of behavior and interactions. These boundaries serve as a way to protect our well-being and maintain a sense of self-respect and dignity. Without clear boundaries, it is easy to become overwhelmed and feel taken advantage of, leading to stress, resentment, and disharmony in relationships.

In a professional setting, setting boundaries is essential for establishing a healthy work environment and maintaining a sense of professionalism. This can include setting limits on the amount of work you take on, defining how you will be treated by colleagues and superiors, and establishing clear lines of communication. By setting boundaries, you are able to protect your time and energy, avoid burnout, and establish a sense of autonomy and control over your work life. Additionally, setting boundaries can help to foster respect and trust among colleagues, as they come to understand and respect your needs and limitations.

In personal relationships, setting boundaries is equally important for maintaining healthy dynamics and fostering respectful interactions. This can include defining what behavior is acceptable in a relationship, establishing limits on how time and resources are shared, and communicating your needs and preferences to others. By setting boundaries, you are able to protect your emotional well-being, maintain a sense of autonomy and self-respect, and ensure that your needs are met in the relationship. Boundaries also help to prevent misunderstandings and conflicts, as they provide a clear framework for how individuals should interact with one another.

Setting boundaries is not about building walls or shutting others out, but rather about establishing clear and respectful guidelines for how you expect to be treated and how you will engage with others. It is a way of asserting yourself and taking ownership of your needs and desires, while also respecting the needs and boundaries of others. By setting boundaries, you are able to create a safe and supportive space in which relationships can thrive and grow, free from manipulation, disrespect, and conflict.

Setting boundaries can be a challenging process, especially if you are not used to asserting yourself or are worried about upsetting others. However, it is important to remember that setting boundaries is a healthy and necessary part of establishing relationships based on mutual respect and understanding. It is okay to say no, to speak up about what you need, and to assert yourself in a calm and respectful manner. By setting boundaries, you are not only taking care of yourself, but also creating a space in which healthy and fulfilling relationships can flourish.

In order to set boundaries effectively, it is important to be clear and specific about what you need and expect from others. This may involve having difficult conversations, setting limits on your time and energy, and being assertive in expressing your needs and preferences. It can be helpful to practice assertiveness techniques, such as using "I" statements to communicate your feelings and needs, setting limits on what you are willing to accept from others, and being firm and consistent in your boundaries. By setting clear and consistent boundaries, you are able to establish a sense of trust and respect in your relationships, and create a healthy and supportive environment in which all parties can thrive.

- Implementing consequences

Implementing consequences is a crucial aspect of behavioral management in various settings, including schools, workplaces, and even within families. Consequences help to reinforce desired behaviors and discourage unwanted behaviors by linking actions to outcomes. By clearly outlining the consequences of certain actions, individuals are more likely to make informed decisions and take responsibility for their behavior. However, it is important to establish consequences that are fair, consistent, and appropriate to the situation in order to effectively modify behavior.

When implementing consequences, it is essential to consider the context in which the behavior occurs. Different settings may require different approaches to consequences based on the specific norms and expectations of that environment. For example, consequences in a classroom setting may involve loss of privileges or a warning system, whereas consequences in a workplace setting may involve formal disciplinary action or performance reviews. By tailoring consequences to the specific setting, individuals are more likely to understand the expectations and consequences of their behavior.

In addition to considering the context of the behavior, it is important to ensure that consequences are fair and proportional to the action. Punitive consequences that are disproportionate to the behavior can lead to feelings of resentment and may not effectively modify behavior in the long term. On the other hand, consequences that are too lenient may not serve as a deterrent to unwanted behavior. By striking a balance between fairness and proportionality, consequences can effectively reinforce positive behavior and discourage negative behavior.

Consistency is another key aspect of implementing consequences. In order for consequences to be effective, they must be consistently applied across all individuals and situations. Inconsistency in consequences can lead to confusion and resentment among those subject to the consequences, as well as undermine the credibility of the system. By establishing clear guidelines and consequences that are consistently enforced, individuals are more likely to understand the expectations and consequences of their behavior, leading to a more positive and productive environment.

It is also important to ensure that consequences are appropriate to the situation and the individual. What may be considered an appropriate consequence for one individual may not be as effective for another. Factors such as age, maturity, and personal circumstances should be taken into account when determining consequences. It is essential to consider the individual's perspective and provide opportunities for dialogue and reflection in order to ensure that consequences are meaningful and effective in changing behavior.

By considering the context, fairness, consistency, and appropriateness of consequences, individuals are more likely to understand the expectations and consequences of their behavior. By establishing clear guidelines and consequences that are consistently applied, individuals can take responsibility for their actions and make informed decisions in order to foster a positive and productive environment.

- Practicing positive discipline

Positive discipline is a parenting approach that focuses on teaching children appropriate behavior through positive reinforcement and guidance. It is based on the belief that children learn best when they are treated with kindness, respect, and understanding. Positive discipline encourages parents to set clear expectations and boundaries for their children, while also providing them with the tools and skills they need to meet those expectations. By using positive discipline techniques, parents can help their children develop self-control, responsibility, and problem-solving skills.

One of the key principles of positive discipline is the importance of building a strong and positive relationship with your child. This means taking the time to listen to your child, validate their feelings, and show empathy and understanding. By fostering a loving and supportive relationship with your child, you can create a foundation of trust and mutual respect that will help them feel safe and secure in their environment. When children feel valued and respected, they are more likely to cooperate and follow the rules.

Another important aspect of positive discipline is setting clear and consistent boundaries for your child. Children thrive on structure and routine, and having clear rules and expectations can help them feel safe and secure. It is important to communicate these boundaries in a calm and respectful manner, and to enforce them consistently. When children understand what is expected of them and what the consequences will be for their actions, they are more likely to follow the rules and behave appropriately.

Positive discipline also emphasizes the importance of teaching children problem-solving skills. Instead of simply punishing children for misbehavior, positive discipline encourages parents to help their children understand why their behavior was unacceptable and to help them come up with alternative solutions. By involving children in the problem-solving process, parents can empower them to take responsibility for their actions and learn from their mistakes. This approach helps children develop critical thinking skills and the ability to make better choices in the future.

In addition to teaching problem-solving skills, positive discipline also encourages parents to focus on reinforcing positive behavior. This means praising and rewarding children when they exhibit good behavior, rather than only focusing on correcting negative behavior. By noticing and acknowledging when children are behaving well, parents can help motivate them to continue making positive choices. This positive reinforcement can help children develop self-confidence and a sense of accomplishment, which can in turn lead to improved behavior. By using these techniques, parents can help their children develop the self-control, responsibility, and social skills they need to succeed in life. Positive discipline is a respectful and effective approach to parenting that can lead to happier and healthier relationships between parents and children. By focusing on building a strong and positive connection with your child, setting clear and consistent boundaries, teaching problem-solving skills, and reinforcing positive behavior, you can help your child grow into a confident and responsible individual.

Chapter 10: Fostering social skills

- TEACHING EMPATHY

Teaching empathy is a crucial aspect of education and personal development that should not be overlooked. Empathy is the ability to understand and share the feelings of others, and it plays a significant role in building positive relationships, resolving conflicts, and fostering a sense of community. In today's fast-paced and interconnected world, cultivating empathy is more important than ever. As educators, it is our responsibility to instill empathy in our students and help them develop the skills needed to navigate social interactions with compassion and understanding.

One of the key ways to teach empathy is through modeling behavior. Children learn by observing the actions and reactions of those around them, so it is essential for teachers to demonstrate empathy in their own interactions. This can be as simple as listening actively to students, acknowledging their feelings, and validating their experiences. By showing empathy towards students, teachers can create a safe and supportive environment where students feel understood and cared for. This in turn encourages students to practice empathy towards their peers, fostering a culture of kindness and respect in the classroom.

Another effective way to teach empathy is through perspective-taking activities. Encouraging students to see things from different points of view helps them develop a deeper understanding of others' feelings and experiences. Role-playing exercises, literature discussions, and group projects can all be used to help students empathize with characters or people from diverse backgrounds. By engaging in these activities, students learn to appreciate the complexity of human emotions and develop their capacity for empathy towards others.

It is also important to explicitly teach empathy skills to students. This can be done through lessons and discussions that focus on empathy, emotional intelligence, and effective communication. Teaching students how to recognize and express their own emotions, as well as how to respond sensitively to the emotions of others, can help them develop strong empathy skills. Role-playing scenarios, practicing active listening, and engaging in reflective writing exercises are all valuable tools for teaching empathy and fostering emotional intelligence in students.

In addition to in-class activities, incorporating empathy into the curriculum can help reinforce the importance of empathy in all areas of students' lives. Reading literature that explores themes of empathy and compassion, studying historical events from multiple perspectives, and discussing real-world issues that require empathy and understanding can all help students see the relevance of empathy in their academic and personal pursuits. By integrating empathy into the curriculum, teachers can show students that empathy is not just a soft skill, but a critical component of their success and well-being.

Ultimately, teaching empathy is about nurturing a culture of empathy in the classroom and beyond. By creating a supportive and inclusive learning environment, modeling empathetic behavior, and providing opportunities for students to practice and develop their empathy skills, educators can help students become more compassionate, understanding, and responsible members of society. Empathy is not just a feel-good quality; it is a vital skill that can help students succeed academically, socially, and emotionally. By prioritizing empathy in education, we can help build a more compassionate and connected world for future generations.

- Encouraging teamwork

Teamwork is a crucial component of any successful organization, as it allows individuals to come together to achieve shared goals and objectives. Encouraging teamwork within a group can lead to increased productivity, enhanced creativity, and improved communication among team members. By fostering a culture of collaboration and cooperation, organizations can harness the collective strengths and talents of their employees to drive innovation and achieve success.

One of the key ways to encourage teamwork within a group is to establish clear goals and expectations. When team members have a shared understanding of what they are working towards and what is expected of them, they are more likely to come together to achieve those goals. By setting measurable and achievable targets, team members can track their progress and stay motivated to work together towards a common purpose.

Another important aspect of fostering teamwork is to promote open communication among team members. When individuals feel comfortable sharing their thoughts, ideas, and concerns with one another, it creates a sense of trust and camaraderie within the group. Encouraging active listening and respectful dialogue can help team members better understand each other's perspectives and collaborate more effectively towards a common goal.

Building a sense of trust and mutual respect among team members is essential for promoting teamwork. When individuals feel valued and respected by their peers, they are more likely to work together in a constructive and supportive manner. Encouraging team-building activities, such as group outings or workshops, can help foster positive relationships and strengthen the bonds between team members.

Effective leadership is also critical in encouraging teamwork within a group. A strong leader can inspire and motivate team members to work together towards a common goal, providing guidance and support when needed. By creating a positive work environment and leading by example, leaders can set the tone for collaboration and cooperation among team members.

Recognizing and rewarding teamwork is another important strategy for encouraging collaboration within a group. When individuals are acknowledged for their contributions and efforts towards the team's goals, it motivates them to continue working together towards success. By celebrating team achievements and highlighting the importance of collaboration, organizations can reinforce the value of teamwork and inspire team members to continue working together towards shared objectives. By establishing clear goals, promoting open communication, building trust and mutual respect, providing effective leadership, and recognizing and rewarding teamwork, organizations can create a collaborative work environment where team members can come together to achieve their shared objectives. When individuals work together towards a common purpose, they can leverage their collective strengths and talents to overcome challenges, drive innovation, and achieve success. Ultimately, fostering teamwork within a group is key to building a strong and resilient organization that can adapt and thrive in today's rapidly changing business landscape.

- Handling social situations

Social situations can be challenging for many people, as they require navigating complex social norms, expectations, and dynamics. In order to handle social situations effectively, it is important to develop strong communication skills, emotional intelligence, and social awareness. By understanding and practicing these skills, individuals can feel more confident and comfortable in various social settings.

One key aspect of handling social situations is effective communication. This involves not only being able to express oneself clearly and effectively, but also being able to listen attentively and respond appropriately to others. In social situations, it is important to be mindful of both verbal and nonverbal cues, such as body language, tone of voice, and facial expressions. By paying attention to these cues, individuals can better understand the thoughts and feelings of those around them, and adjust their own communication style accordingly.

Emotional intelligence is another important skill to develop when handling social situations. This involves being able to recognize and manage one's own emotions, as well as being empathetic and sensitive to the emotions of others. By being able to regulate emotions and respond in a calm and rational manner, individuals can navigate social interactions more effectively and build stronger relationships with others. Developing emotional intelligence also involves being able to recognize and understand the emotions of others, and respond in a way that is supportive and empathetic.

Social awareness is also crucial when it comes to handling social situations. This involves being able to understand and navigate social dynamics, norms, and expectations. By being aware of social cues, norms, and expectations, individuals can better adapt their behavior and communication style to fit the context. This can help individuals avoid misunderstandings, conflicts, or social faux pas, and build positive relationships with others. Developing social awareness also involves being able to read social situations accurately, and respond in a way that is appropriate and respectful.

In order to handle social situations effectively, it is important to practice and refine these skills in various social settings. This may involve stepping out of one's comfort zone, trying new social activities, or seeking out opportunities to practice and improve social skills. By challenging oneself and pushing past any social anxieties or fears, individuals can build confidence and competence in handling social situations. It is also important to seek feedback from others, such as friends, family members, or mentors, in order to gain insight into one's social skills and areas for improvement. By developing and practicing these skills, individuals can feel more confident, comfortable, and successful in a variety of social settings. Through practice, feedback, and self-reflection, individuals can continue to improve their social skills and build positive relationships with others. By approaching social situations with an open mind, a willingness to learn, and a positive attitude, individuals can navigate social interactions with grace and ease.

Chapter 11: Coping with emotional struggles

- UNDERSTANDING EMOTIONS

Emotions play a crucial role in shaping our daily experiences and interactions with the world around us. They guide our decision-making processes, influence our social interactions, and impact our physical and mental well-being. Understanding emotions involves delving into the complex and multifaceted nature of human emotions, exploring the underlying mechanisms that drive them, and learning how to effectively manage and regulate them.

One of the key aspects of understanding emotions is recognizing that they are not purely subjective experiences, but rather a complex interplay of biological, psychological, and social factors. Emotions are rooted in the brain and are governed by a complex network of neural circuits and chemical messengers. For example, the amygdala, a small almond-shaped region in the brain, is known to play a crucial role in processing emotional stimuli and triggering the body's fight-or-flight response to perceived threats. In addition, neurotransmitters such as dopamine, serotonin, and norepinephrine are involved in regulating mood and emotional states.

However, emotions are not solely determined by biological factors. They are also shaped by our past experiences, beliefs, values, and cultural norms. For example, someone who has had a negative experience in the past may be more prone to feeling anxious or fearful in similar situations in the future. Similarly, cultural norms and societal expectations can influence how emotions are expressed and perceived. In some cultures, openly displaying emotions such as anger or sadness may be frowned upon, while in others, emotional expression is encouraged and valued.

Another important aspect of understanding emotions is recognizing the role of cognitive processes in shaping our emotional experiences. Our thoughts, beliefs, and interpretations of events can significantly influence how we feel and respond to situations. For example, someone who tends to catastrophize or engage in negative self-talk may be more prone to experiencing heightened levels of anxiety or depression. On the other hand, individuals who practice cognitive restructuring and focus on more balanced and realistic interpretations of events may be better able to regulate their emotions and maintain a more positive outlook.

Emotions are also inherently social phenomena, as they are often expressed and experienced in the context of our relationships with others. Social interactions play a crucial role in shaping our emotional experiences, as they provide opportunities for emotional expression, validation, and support. For example, sharing our feelings with a trusted friend or family member can help us feel heard, understood, and supported, which can in turn help us regulate our emotions and cope with difficult situations. Conversely, social rejection or conflict can trigger negative emotions such as sadness, anger, or loneliness.

Understanding emotions also involves learning how to effectively manage and regulate them. Emotion regulation refers to the ability to monitor, evaluate, and modulate one's emotional responses in order to achieve desired outcomes. This involves a range of strategies, from simple techniques such as deep breathing and mindfulness to more complex cognitive and behavioral interventions. For example, cognitive reappraisal involves reframing a situation in a more positive or neutral light in order to reduce negative emotional responses. Similarly, behavioral strategies such as distraction or problem-solving can help individuals cope with difficult emotions and make more adaptive choices. By gaining insight into the underlying mechanisms that drive emotions, recognizing the role of cognitive processes in shaping our emotional responses, and learning effective strategies for managing and regulating emotions, we can enhance our emotional intelligence, improve our relationships, and foster greater well-being and resilience. Emotions are an integral part of the human experience, and developing a better understanding of them can empower us to navigate the ups and downs of life with greater ease and mindfulness.

- Teaching coping skills

Coping skills are an essential aspect of mental health and well-being, particularly in our fast-paced and demanding society. Teaching coping skills to individuals can equip them with the tools they need to navigate life's challenges and stressors effectively. Coping skills are strategies that individuals use to manage and cope with difficult situations, emotions, and stress. These skills can range from simple relaxation techniques to more complex problem-solving strategies. By teaching coping skills, individuals can improve their resilience, emotional regulation, and overall mental well-being.

One of the key benefits of teaching coping skills is that it can help individuals develop a sense of control over their emotions and reactions. When faced with a stressful or challenging situation, individuals who possess effective coping skills are better able to manage their emotions and respond in a calm and rational manner. This can help prevent feelings of overwhelm, panic, or helplessness, and instead empower individuals to take control of the situation and find constructive solutions. By teaching coping skills, individuals can learn how to regulate their emotions and behavior, leading to improved mental and emotional well-being.

Another important aspect of teaching coping skills is that it can help individuals build resilience in the face of adversity. Resilience is the ability to bounce back from setbacks and challenges, and it is an important component of mental health and well-being. By teaching coping skills, individuals can learn how to adapt and cope with difficult situations, enabling them to overcome obstacles and setbacks more effectively. Developing resilience through coping skills can help individuals become more resourceful, adaptable, and confident in their ability to face life's challenges with resilience and determination.

Additionally, teaching coping skills can help individuals improve their problem-solving abilities. Coping skills are not only about managing emotions and stress, but also about finding practical solutions to difficult situations. By teaching individuals how to effectively cope with stress and challenges, they can develop better problem-solving skills and strategies. This can enable them to approach difficult situations with a clear and rational mind, allowing them to identify and implement effective solutions. By teaching coping skills that incorporate problem-solving techniques, individuals can enhance their ability to find creative, practical, and effective solutions to the challenges they face.

Furthermore, teaching coping skills can help individuals improve their relationships and communication with others. Effective coping skills can help individuals manage their emotions and reactions in social situations, leading to better communication, conflict resolution, and interpersonal relationships. By understanding and utilizing coping skills, individuals can develop better emotional intelligence, empathy, and conflict resolution abilities. This can lead to healthier and more positive relationships with others, as well as improved communication and collaboration in personal and professional settings. By teaching coping skills that focus on interpersonal communication and conflict resolution, individuals can enhance their social and emotional intelligence, leading to stronger and more fulfilling relationships. By providing individuals with the tools and strategies they need to manage stress, regulate emotions, build resilience, solve problems, and improve relationships, teaching coping skills can help individuals thrive in the face of life's challenges. Coping skills are invaluable assets that can empower individuals to navigate difficult situations with grace, confidence, and resilience. By teaching coping skills in a comprehensive and supportive manner, individuals can enhance their emotional well-being, interpersonal relationships, problem-solving abilities, and resilience, leading to a happier and more fulfilling life.

- Supporting mental health

Supporting mental health is crucial for overall well-being and quality of life. Mental health refers to our emotional, psychological, and social well-being, and it affects how we think, feel, and act. Just like physical health, mental health is essential for our day-to-day functioning and our ability to cope with stress, make decisions, form relationships, and achieve our goals. It is important to prioritize mental health and provide support for those who may be struggling with mental health challenges.

There are various ways to support mental health, including seeking professional help, building supportive relationships, engaging in self-care practices, and promoting mental health awareness and education. One of the most effective ways to support mental health is to seek assistance from mental health professionals such as therapists, psychologists, and psychiatrists. These experts can provide therapy, medication management, and other interventions to help individuals manage their mental health symptoms and improve their overall well-being.

In addition to professional help, building supportive relationships can also play a crucial role in supporting mental health. Having a strong support network of family, friends, and peers can provide emotional support, encouragement, and a sense of belonging, which can help individuals cope with the challenges of mental health issues. By maintaining open and honest communication with loved ones, individuals can feel understood, validated, and supported in their mental health journey.

Engaging in self-care practices is another important way to support mental health. Self-care involves taking care of one's physical, emotional, and mental well-being by practicing activities that promote relaxation, mindfulness, and stress reduction. This can include activities such as exercise, meditation, journaling, spending time in nature, and engaging in hobbies and interests. By prioritizing self-care and making time for activities that bring joy and relaxation, individuals can improve their mental health and overall well-being.

Furthermore, promoting mental health awareness and education is essential for creating a supportive and stigma-free environment for individuals struggling with mental health challenges. By increasing awareness about mental health issues, reducing stigma, and providing information about available resources and support services, we can encourage individuals to seek help and support when needed. Education about mental health can also help individuals recognize the signs and symptoms of mental health issues in themselves and others, leading to early intervention and better outcomes. By seeking professional help, building supportive relationships, engaging in self-care practices, and promoting mental health awareness and education, we can create a supportive environment for individuals struggling with mental health challenges. It is important to prioritize mental health and provide the necessary support and resources to help individuals manage their mental health symptoms and improve their overall well-being. Let us strive to create a more understanding and compassionate society that values mental health and supports those in need.

Chapter 12: Nurturing physical health

- ENCOURAGING EXERCISE

Exercise is a crucial component of maintaining a healthy lifestyle, yet many individuals struggle to incorporate regular physical activity into their daily routines. Encouraging exercise not only has physical benefits, such as improving cardiovascular health, enhancing muscle strength, and promoting weight management, but it also has numerous psychological benefits, such as reducing stress, improving mood, and boosting self-esteem. Therefore, it is essential for individuals to find ways to make exercise a priority in their lives to reap these many benefits.

One way to encourage exercise is to find activities that are enjoyable and engaging. While some people may find running on a treadmill or lifting weights at the gym to be monotonous, others may find pleasure in dancing, hiking, or playing team sports. By exploring different types of physical activities, individuals can discover what truly brings them joy and fulfillment, making it more likely that they will stick with their exercise routine in the long term. Additionally, finding a workout buddy or joining a group fitness class can provide social support and accountability, making exercise more enjoyable and motivating.

Another important factor in encouraging exercise is setting realistic and achievable goals. Many individuals may become discouraged when they set overly ambitious goals, such as running a marathon or losing a significant amount of weight in a short period of time. Instead, setting smaller, more attainable goals, such as walking for 30 minutes a day or completing a beginner's yoga class once a week, can help individuals build confidence and momentum in their fitness journey. By celebrating small victories along the way, individuals can stay motivated and committed to their exercise regimen.

Creating a structured and consistent exercise routine is also essential for encouraging regular physical activity. Just as individuals schedule time for work, meals, and social activities, they should prioritize exercise as an integral part of their daily or weekly schedule. Whether it's waking up early for a morning jog, taking a lunchtime walk break, or attending an evening yoga class, establishing a routine can help individuals develop a habit of exercising regularly. Additionally, varying the types of exercises and intensities can prevent boredom and plateaus, keeping individuals engaged and motivated in their fitness routine.

Incorporating physical activity into daily tasks and routines can also make it easier to stay active throughout the day. Simple changes, such as taking the stairs instead of the elevator, walking or biking to work or school, or doing bodyweight exercises during commercial breaks, can add up to significant amounts of physical activity over time. By finding creative ways to move more and sit less throughout the day, individuals can increase their overall levels of physical activity without requiring additional time or effort.

Furthermore, finding ways to make exercise convenient and accessible can remove barriers and excuses that may prevent individuals from being active. Investing in home workout equipment, finding online workout videos, or utilizing fitness apps can make it easier for individuals to exercise in the comfort of their own homes. Joining a local gym, recreation center, or fitness class can provide access to equipment and facilities that support various types of physical activities. By finding convenient and accessible options for exercise, individuals can eliminate logistical challenges and make it easier to prioritize their health and well-being.

Lastly, it is important for individuals to listen to their bodies and prioritize rest and recovery as part of their overall fitness routine. Pushing oneself too hard or neglecting rest days can lead to burnout, injury, or decreased motivation to exercise. By incorporating stretching, foam rolling, meditation, or other forms of restorative practices into their routine, individuals can support their physical and mental well-being, allowing them to exercise more effectively and sustainably. Furthermore, seeking guidance from fitness professionals, such as personal trainers, physical therapists, or nutritionists, can provide personalized support and advice to help individuals achieve their fitness goals safely and successfully. By finding enjoyable activities, setting realistic goals, establishing a structured routine, integrating exercise into daily tasks, making it convenient and accessible, and prioritizing rest and recovery, individuals can overcome barriers and obstacles to exercise and reap the many benefits of an active lifestyle. By taking small steps and making gradual changes, individuals can create lasting habits that support their health and fitness goals for the long term.

- Promoting healthy eating habits

It is essential for individuals to consume a balanced diet that provides the necessary nutrients for optimal functioning of the body. Healthy eating habits not only impact physical health but also mental and emotional well-being.

One of the key components of promoting healthy eating habits is education. By providing individuals with information about the importance of nutrition and the benefits of consuming a balanced diet, people can make more informed choices when it comes to their food selections. This can be done through educational programs, workshops, and seminars that focus on topics such as the food groups, portion control, and reading nutrition labels.

In addition to education, it is important to create a supportive environment that encourages healthy eating habits. This can be done by making healthy food options easily accessible, such as offering a variety of fruits and vegetables in workplace cafeterias or schools. By providing healthy options, individuals are more likely to choose nutritious foods over less healthy alternatives. Additionally, creating a social support network can also be beneficial in promoting healthy eating habits. By engaging in activities such as cooking classes or group meal planning, individuals can receive support and encouragement from others who are also striving to make positive changes to their diet.

Another effective strategy for promoting healthy eating habits is to develop personalized meal plans. By working with a nutritionist or dietitian, individuals can receive guidance on creating a meal plan that meets their specific nutritional needs and goals. This can help individuals establish a routine for meal planning and preparation, making it easier to consistently consume a balanced diet. By incorporating a variety of foods from all food groups, individuals can ensure they are receiving the necessary nutrients for optimal health.

It is important to recognize that promoting healthy eating habits is not solely about restriction or deprivation. By incorporating moderation and mindfulness into one's eating habits, individuals can maintain a healthy relationship with food and avoid feelings of guilt or shame associated with eating certain foods. It is also important to practice intuitive eating, which involves listening to one's body cues and eating in response to hunger and fullness signals. It is important to remember that healthy eating is a lifelong journey, and it is okay to seek support and guidance along the way. By prioritizing nutrition and making conscious choices when it comes to food, individuals can experience the numerous benefits of a balanced and healthy diet.

- Ensuring adequate sleep

Ensuring adequate sleep is crucial for overall health and well-being. Sleep plays a vital role in various physiological functions, including cognitive performance, emotional regulation, and immune function. However, in today's fast-paced society, many people struggle to get the recommended amount of sleep each night. This can have serious consequences on both physical and mental health.

One of the main reasons why ensuring adequate sleep is important is its impact on cognitive function. Research has shown that sleep plays a crucial role in memory consolidation and learning. When we sleep, our brains process and consolidate information that we have learned throughout the day. This helps to improve our ability to concentrate, make decisions, and solve problems. Inadequate sleep can impair these cognitive functions, leading to decreased productivity and performance in daily activities.

In addition to cognitive function, sleep also plays a crucial role in emotional regulation. Adequate sleep is essential for maintaining a healthy balance of neurotransmitters in the brain, which are responsible for regulating mood and emotions. When we don't get enough sleep, these neurotransmitters can become imbalanced, leading to mood swings, irritability, and increased stress levels. Over time, chronic sleep deprivation can contribute to the development of mental health disorders such as anxiety and depression.

Furthermore, ensuring adequate sleep is important for immune function. During sleep, the body produces and releases cytokines, which are proteins that help regulate the immune response. These cytokines play a key role in fighting off infections and preventing illness. When we don't get enough sleep, our immune system becomes compromised, making us more susceptible to infections and illnesses. In fact, research has shown that people who regularly get less than 7 hours of sleep per night are more likely to get sick than those who get an adequate amount of sleep.

Given the importance of ensuring adequate sleep, it is essential to prioritize good sleep habits and establish a consistent sleep routine. This includes going to bed and waking up at the same time every day, even on weekends, to regulate the body's internal clock. Creating a relaxing bedtime routine, such as reading a book or taking a warm bath, can help signal to the body that it is time to wind down and prepare for sleep.

It is also important to create a sleep-friendly environment by ensuring that the bedroom is cool, dark, and quiet. Investing in a comfortable mattress and pillows can also help improve sleep quality. Additionally, avoiding stimulants such as caffeine and electronic devices close to bedtime can help promote a restful night's sleep. Sleep plays a crucial role in cognitive function, emotional regulation, and immune function. By prioritizing good sleep habits and establishing a consistent sleep routine, we can improve our sleep quality and reduce the risk of developing health issues associated with chronic sleep deprivation. If you are struggling to get enough sleep, consider speaking with a healthcare professional for personalized guidance and support. Remember, a good night's sleep is a key component of a healthy lifestyle.

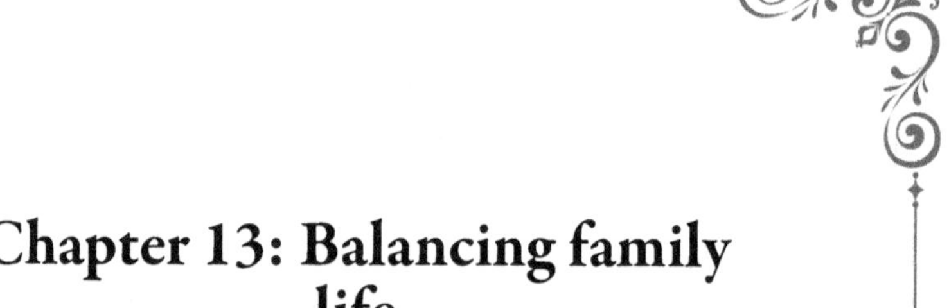

Chapter 13: Balancing family life

- MANAGING SIBLING RELATIONSHIPS

Managing sibling relationships can be a challenging task that requires patience, understanding, and effective communication. Siblings share a unique bond that is often characterized by a mix of love, rivalry, and loyalty. While sibling relationships can be incredibly rewarding, they can also be fraught with conflict and tension. In order to foster healthy and positive relationships with siblings, it is important to establish boundaries, respect each other's differences, and prioritize open and honest communication.

One of the key aspects of managing sibling relationships is setting clear boundaries. Boundaries help to establish mutual respect and prevent conflicts from escalating. It is important for siblings to establish boundaries around personal space, belongings, and time. By clearly communicating and respecting each other's boundaries, siblings can create a harmonious and respectful relationship that is built on trust and understanding. Setting boundaries also helps to prevent misunderstandings and disagreements, as each sibling knows what is expected of them and what is off-limits.

Respecting each other's differences is another crucial element in managing sibling relationships. Siblings are unique individuals with their own personalities, interests, and perspectives. It is important to respect and celebrate these differences, rather than trying to mold each other into a certain mold. By recognizing and accepting each other's differences, siblings can foster a sense of acceptance and understanding that strengthens their bond. Respecting each other's differences also means refraining from judgment and criticism, and instead focusing on empathy and compassion. By embracing each other's uniqueness, siblings can create a supportive and inclusive environment where they can thrive and grow together.

Open and honest communication is essential in managing sibling relationships. Communication is the foundation of any healthy relationship, and siblings are no exception. It is important for siblings to communicate openly and honestly with each other, expressing their thoughts, feelings, and needs in a respectful and constructive manner. Effective communication helps to resolve conflicts, prevent misunderstandings, and build trust and understanding between siblings. By fostering open and honest communication, siblings can create a strong and enduring bond that is based on mutual respect and support. It is also important for siblings to listen actively and attentively to each other, showing empathy and understanding towards each other's perspectives and feelings.

In addition to setting boundaries, respecting differences, and fostering open communication, it is important for siblings to prioritize quality time together. Spending quality time with siblings helps to strengthen the bond between them and create lasting memories. Whether it's going for a walk, sharing a meal, or engaging in a favorite activity together, spending quality time with siblings can help to deepen the connection and strengthen the relationship. Quality time together also provides an opportunity for siblings to communicate, laugh, and create positive experiences that build a sense of togetherness and unity. By setting boundaries, respecting differences, fostering open and honest communication, and prioritizing quality time together, siblings can build strong and meaningful relationships that stand the test of time. Siblings share a unique bond that can be both challenging and rewarding, and by investing time and effort into managing their relationships, siblings can create a supportive and loving environment where they can thrive and grow together. Ultimately, sibling relationships are an important part of our lives, and by nurturing and managing these relationships effectively, siblings can create a lasting and enduring bond that enriches their lives and brings them joy and fulfillment.

- Prioritizing self-care

Self-care is a vital aspect of maintaining overall well-being and mental health. It involves taking intentional actions to care for oneself physically, emotionally, mentally, and spiritually. In today's fast-paced and demanding world, it is easy to neglect our own needs in favor of work, family, or other obligations. However, prioritizing self-care is essential for our overall health and happiness.

One of the first steps in prioritizing self-care is recognizing the importance of taking care of oneself. Often, we are conditioned to put others' needs ahead of our own, believing that self-care is selfish or indulgent. However, self-care is not only necessary but also beneficial for both ourselves and those around us. When we neglect our own needs, we may become burnt out, stressed, or unhappy, which can negatively impact our relationships and performance in other areas of our lives. By prioritizing self-care, we are better able to show up as our best selves for others and meet our obligations with a sense of balance and fulfillment.

There are many different ways to prioritize self-care, and what works best for one person may not work for another. It is important to experiment with different self-care practices and find what resonates with you personally. Some common self-care activities include exercise, meditation, journaling, spending time in nature, engaging in hobbies or creative pursuits, and connecting with loved ones. By incorporating a variety of self-care practices into your routine, you can ensure that you are addressing your physical, emotional, mental, and spiritual well-being.

Setting boundaries is another key aspect of prioritizing self-care. It is important to recognize when you are taking on too much and learn to say no to additional responsibilities or commitments when necessary. Setting boundaries with others may feel uncomfortable at first, but it is crucial for protecting your own well-being and ensuring that you have time and energy to devote to self-care. By setting clear boundaries and communicating your needs to others, you can create a more balanced and sustainable lifestyle that prioritizes your own needs.

It is also important to practice self-compassion when prioritizing self-care. We often hold ourselves to high standards and may be overly self-critical when we fall short of our own expectations. It is important to treat ourselves with the same kindness and understanding that we would offer to a friend. Self-compassion involves recognizing our own humanity, acknowledging our imperfections, and offering ourselves support and encouragement in times of need. By practicing self-compassion, we can cultivate a more positive and nurturing relationship with ourselves, which can have a profound impact on our overall well-being.

In addition to individual self-care practices, it is important to prioritize self-care on a broader societal level. This includes advocating for policies and practices that support work-life balance, mental health resources, and access to quality healthcare. By promoting a culture that values self-care and well-being, we can create more supportive and sustainable environments for everyone. Prioritizing self-care is not only an individual responsibility but also a collective effort to create healthier and more resilient communities. By recognizing the importance of self-care, experimenting with different self-care practices, setting boundaries, practicing self-compassion, and advocating for supportive policies and practices, we can create a more balanced and fulfilling life for ourselves and those around us. Self-care is not a luxury but a necessity, and by making it a priority, we can ensure that we are living our best lives and contributing positively to the world around us.

- Finding time for family activities

Finding time for family activities in today's fast-paced world can be a challenging task, but it is essential for maintaining strong bonds and creating lasting memories with loved ones. With busy work schedules, school commitments, extracurricular activities, and other obligations, it can be easy for families to become overwhelmed and neglect the importance of spending quality time together. However, prioritizing family time and making a conscious effort to plan and engage in activities together can have numerous benefits for both parents and children.

One of the first steps in finding time for family activities is recognizing the importance of doing so. Research has consistently shown that families who spend time together engaging in meaningful activities have stronger relationships, better communication, and a greater sense of unity. These positive outcomes can have a lasting impact on children's emotional and social development, as well as their overall well-being. By acknowledging the value of family time, parents can begin to prioritize it in their schedules and make it a non-negotiable part of their daily or weekly routine.

Another key aspect of finding time for family activities is effective time management. With so many demands on our time, it can be challenging to carve out dedicated moments for family togetherness. However, with proper planning and organization, it is possible to create pockets of time for shared activities. Setting aside specific days or times each week for family outings or activities can help ensure that they do not get lost amid the hustle and bustle of everyday life. By creating a family calendar and coordinating schedules, parents can identify opportunities for quality time and make the most of them.

Additionally, making the most of everyday moments can also help families find time for activities together. Simple activities such as cooking a meal together, going for a walk in the neighborhood, or playing board games can be enjoyable ways to connect and bond as a family without requiring a significant time commitment. By incorporating these small but meaningful moments into their daily routine, parents can ensure that family time becomes a regular and cherished part of their lives.

Furthermore, incorporating family activities into special occasions and holidays can also be a great way to create lasting memories and strengthen family bonds. Whether it's celebrating birthdays, holidays, or other significant events, parents can use these opportunities to plan fun and engaging activities that everyone can enjoy together. This not only adds excitement and joy to special occasions but also reinforces the importance of spending time together as a family and making the most of the moments you have with your loved ones.

Despite the challenges of finding time for family activities, it is important for parents to remember that the benefits far outweigh the difficulties. By prioritizing family time, planning and organizing activities, making the most of everyday moments, and incorporating family activities into special occasions, parents can create a strong sense of connection and togetherness that will last a lifetime. Ultimately, investing in quality time with your family is an investment in your relationships, your children's well-being, and the overall health and happiness of your family unit. So, take the time to plan and prioritize family activities, and watch as your relationships flourish and your family bond grows stronger with each passing day.

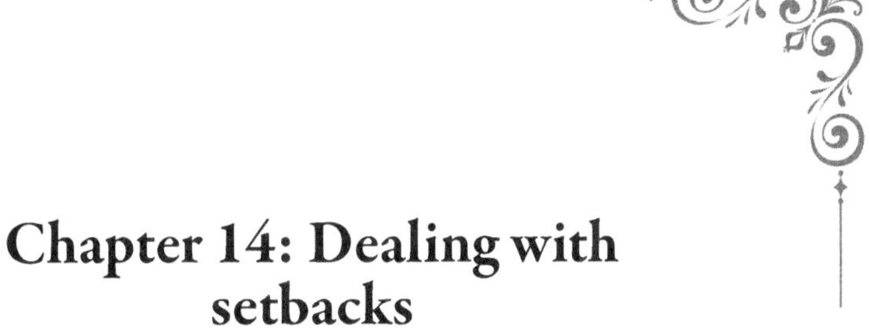

Chapter 14: Dealing with setbacks

- OVERCOMING OBSTACLES

Overcoming obstacles is a common theme in human experience, as individuals often face challenges and setbacks that can hinder their progress and success. These obstacles can come in many forms, including personal limitations, external circumstances, or unforeseen events. However, by developing and implementing strategies to overcome these obstacles, individuals can achieve their goals and fulfill their potential.

One key strategy for overcoming obstacles is to maintain a positive mindset and attitude. By staying optimistic and focusing on potential solutions rather than dwelling on problems, individuals can effectively navigate challenges and setbacks. This positive mindset can help individuals persist in the face of adversity, maintain motivation, and find creative solutions to obstacles. Research has shown that individuals who maintain a positive attitude are more likely to overcome obstacles and achieve their goals.

Another important strategy for overcoming obstacles is to develop resilience and adaptability. Resilience refers to the ability to bounce back from setbacks and challenges, while adaptability refers to the ability to adjust to changing circumstances. By developing resilience and adaptability, individuals can effectively overcome obstacles and thrive in the face of adversity. Research has shown that individuals who are resilient and adaptable are better able to overcome obstacles and achieve their goals.

In addition to maintaining a positive mindset and developing resilience and adaptability, individuals can also benefit from seeking support from others.

Whether it be friends, family, mentors, or professional support, having a strong support network can provide individuals with encouragement, guidance, and resources to help them overcome obstacles. Research has shown that individuals who receive support from others are more likely to overcome obstacles and achieve their goals.

Furthermore, individuals can benefit from setting realistic goals and developing a clear plan of action to overcome obstacles. By setting specific, measurable, attainable, relevant, and time-bound goals, individuals can focus their efforts and resources on overcoming obstacles in a systematic and organized manner. Research has shown that individuals who set clear goals and develop a plan of action are more likely to overcome obstacles and achieve their goals. By maintaining a positive mindset, developing resilience and adaptability, seeking support from others, and setting realistic goals and developing a clear plan of action, individuals can effectively overcome obstacles and achieve their goals. With determination, persistence, and a willingness to learn and grow from setbacks, individuals can navigate challenges and setbacks and emerge stronger and more resilient than before.

- Reassessing strategies

In today's rapidly changing and dynamic business environment, it has become increasingly essential for organizations to regularly reassess their strategies in order to stay competitive and relevant. The traditional approach of developing a strategic plan and sticking to it for several years has become outdated, as the pace of change in the business world has accelerated significantly. Therefore, it is crucial for businesses to constantly evaluate and adjust their strategies to adapt to these changes and seize new opportunities.

Reassessing strategies involves critically examining the organization's current strategic direction, objectives, and tactics to determine whether they are still aligned with the company's goals and market conditions. This process requires a careful analysis of internal and external factors that may impact the organization's performance, such as changes in technology, customer preferences, regulatory environment, and competitive landscape. By reassessing strategies, companies can identify emerging trends, market shifts, and potential threats that may require them to pivot or refine their approach to remain successful.

One of the key benefits of reassessing strategies is that it enables organizations to stay agile and responsive to changing market conditions. In today's volatile business environment, companies that are able to adapt quickly and effectively to new challenges are more likely to thrive and succeed. By regularly revisiting and adjusting their strategies, businesses can ensure that they are well-positioned to capitalize on new opportunities and address emerging threats. This proactive approach to strategy allows organizations to stay ahead of the curve and maintain a competitive edge in their industry.

Furthermore, reassessing strategies can help organizations identify areas of improvement and innovation that can drive growth and profitability. By critically evaluating their current strategic approach, companies can uncover inefficiencies, bottlenecks, or missed opportunities that may be holding them back. This process of self-assessment can lead to the development of new strategies, initiatives, or business models that can help the organization achieve its long-term objectives and unlock untapped potential. By continuously reassessing and refining their strategies, businesses can foster a culture of innovation and continuous improvement that can propel them to new levels of success.

It is important to note that reassessing strategies is not a one-time event, but rather an ongoing process that should be integrated into the organization's strategic planning and management practices. By building a culture of strategic agility and adaptability, companies can position themselves to navigate uncertainty and change with confidence. This requires a commitment from leadership to prioritize strategic reassessment and empower employees at all levels to contribute ideas and insights that can inform strategic decisions. By regularly evaluating and adjusting their strategic approach, companies can stay agile, responsive, and innovative, positioning themselves for long-term success. This proactive and dynamic approach to strategy is essential for organizations seeking to remain relevant and competitive in an ever-evolving marketplace. Embracing change and uncertainty is key to navigating the challenges and opportunities that lie ahead, and reassessing strategies is a fundamental tool for achieving this goal.

- Seeking additional support

Seeking additional support is an essential step in achieving success and overcoming challenges in various aspects of life. Whether it be in academics, the workplace, or personal relationships, having a support system in place can provide invaluable guidance, encouragement, and resources to help navigate difficult situations. It is important to recognize when one may need additional support and to be proactive in seeking it out in order to effectively address issues and achieve desired outcomes.

In an academic setting, seeking additional support can be particularly beneficial for students who may be struggling with coursework or facing obstacles in their learning journey. This could involve seeking help from teachers, tutors, or academic advisors to clarify concepts, improve study habits, or receive personalized guidance on how to improve academic performance. Additionally, joining study groups or seeking out resources such as library resources, online tutorials or academic workshops can also provide valuable support to enhance learning and academic success.

In the workplace, seeking additional support can be crucial for professional growth and development. This could include seeking mentorship from more experienced colleagues, attending professional development workshops or conferences, or seeking out additional training opportunities to enhance skills and knowledge. It is important to be proactive in seeking support in the workplace in order to advance one's career, build relationships with coworkers, and navigate challenges that may arise in a professional setting.

When facing personal challenges or difficult situations, seeking additional support can also be incredibly beneficial. This could involve reaching out to friends, family members, or seeking support from a therapist or counselor to help navigate feelings of anxiety, depression, or stress. Additionally, joining support groups or engaging in self-care activities such as exercise, mindfulness, or hobbies can also provide valuable support in promoting mental wellbeing and resilience in facing personal challenges. It is important to recognize when one may need additional support and to be proactive in seeking it out in order to effectively address issues and achieve desired outcomes. By cultivating a strong support system and utilizing resources available, individuals can navigate difficulties, overcome obstacles, and ultimately thrive in their personal, academic, and professional pursuits.

Chapter 15: Embracing your child's uniqueness

- CELEBRATING STRENGTHS

Celebrating strengths is an essential component of personal and professional development. By focusing on our strengths, we can build upon our existing abilities and increase our overall effectiveness and satisfaction in various aspects of our lives. Research has shown that individuals who are able to identify and utilize their strengths are more likely to experience success and fulfillment. However, it is also important to acknowledge that everyone has areas of weakness, and that is completely normal. By celebrating our strengths, we are not only recognizing our accomplishments, but we are also gaining confidence and motivation to tackle challenges and improve in areas where we may struggle.

One of the key benefits of celebrating strengths is that it helps to foster a positive mindset. When we focus on our strengths, we are more likely to feel confident and empowered. This positive mindset can have a ripple effect on other areas of our lives, leading to increased motivation and productivity. By acknowledging and celebrating our strengths, we are reinforcing our sense of self-worth and building resilience in the face of obstacles. This can be particularly useful in times of stress or uncertainty, as it can provide us with a sense of purpose and direction.

Another important aspect of celebrating strengths is the impact it can have on our relationships with others. By recognizing and appreciating the strengths of those around us, we can build stronger connections and create a more supportive and uplifting environment. Whether in the workplace, in our personal lives, or within our communities, celebrating each other's strengths can foster collaboration, communication, and mutual respect. When we celebrate the strengths of others, we are not only showing appreciation for their unique abilities, but we are also creating a culture of positivity and encouragement.

In addition to personal and interpersonal benefits, celebrating strengths can also have a significant impact on professional success. By identifying and leveraging our strengths, we can position ourselves for career advancement and growth. When we are able to showcase our strengths, we are more likely to stand out to employers, colleagues, and clients. This can lead to increased opportunities for promotions, collaborations, and networking. By celebrating our strengths, we are also demonstrating our value and expertise in our chosen field, which can help to boost our professional reputation and credibility.

It is important to note that celebrating strengths does not mean ignoring weaknesses or areas for improvement. In fact, by acknowledging our weaknesses and seeking opportunities for growth, we can further enhance our strengths and become more well-rounded individuals. By taking a balanced approach to personal development, we can continue to build upon our strengths while also addressing areas that may need improvement. This comprehensive approach to self-improvement can lead to greater overall success and fulfillment in both our personal and professional lives. By focusing on our strengths, we can boost our confidence, build positive relationships, and increase our chances of success. While it is important to acknowledge our weaknesses and areas for improvement, celebrating our strengths allows us to recognize our unique abilities and talents. By embracing our strengths and striving for continued growth and development, we can unlock our full potential and achieve our goals in a meaningful and fulfilling way. So, let us take the time to celebrate our strengths and those of others, and watch as our lives and relationships flourish as a result.

- Honoring individuality

Individuality is a fundamental aspect of human existence, encompassing a person's unique characteristics, traits, and experiences that set them apart from others. Honoring individuality involves recognizing and respecting the distinctiveness of each person, valuing their personal identity, beliefs, and choices, and celebrating their diversity. Embracing and celebrating individuality is crucial for building a more inclusive and accepting society where everyone feels valued and accepted for who they are.

One of the key aspects of honoring individuality is recognizing the importance of personal autonomy and self-expression. Every individual has the right to express themselves in their own unique way, whether it be through their appearance, beliefs, interests, or lifestyle choices. Respecting and supporting individuals in their self-expression helps to create a sense of freedom and empowerment, enabling them to live authentically and confidently as their true selves. By encouraging and honoring individuality, we can foster a culture of acceptance and understanding that celebrates the richness and diversity of human experience.

Another important aspect of honoring individuality is acknowledging the unique perspectives and contributions that each person brings to the table. Every individual has their own set of skills, talents, and experiences that make them valuable and irreplaceable. By recognizing and appreciating the diverse talents and qualities of individuals, we can create a more inclusive and equitable society that values the contributions of all its members. Honoring individuality in this way promotes creativity, innovation, and collaboration, as different perspectives and ideas are welcomed and respected.

Furthermore, honoring individuality involves recognizing and respecting the boundaries and preferences of others. Each person has their own set of boundaries, comfort levels, and needs that should be acknowledged and respected by others. This includes respecting an individual's personal space, privacy, and decision-making autonomy. By honoring and respecting the boundaries of others, we demonstrate empathy, compassion, and understanding towards their needs and limitations. This contributes to creating a more supportive and inclusive environment where everyone feels safe, valued, and respected.

In addition, honoring individuality involves challenging stereotypes, biases, and prejudices that may limit or restrict an individual's freedom and self-expression. Stereotypes and prejudices are harmful beliefs and attitudes that can lead to discrimination, exclusion, and marginalization of individuals who do not fit societal norms or expectations. By challenging and dismantling stereotypes and prejudices, we can create a more inclusive and equitable society where all individuals are valued and respected for who they are. This requires a commitment to promoting diversity, equity, and social justice, and actively working towards creating a more just and inclusive society for all.

Ultimately, honoring individuality is a continuous and ongoing process that requires a commitment to fostering a culture of acceptance, respect, and celebration of diversity. By valuing and respecting the unique qualities, experiences, and perspectives of each individual, we can create a more inclusive and equitable society where everyone feels seen, heard, and valued. This involves promoting self-expression, celebrating diversity, challenging stereotypes, and respecting the boundaries and preferences of others. By embracing and honoring individuality, we can build a more compassionate, understanding, and accepting society where everyone has the opportunity to thrive and live authentically as their true selves.

- Encouraging interests

Encouraging interests in individuals is a critical aspect of personal and professional development. By fostering curiosity and passion in various areas, individuals are able to explore their talents and strengths, leading to greater fulfillment and success in their lives. Encouraging interests can take many forms, including providing opportunities for exploration, offering support and guidance, and promoting a growth mindset.

One of the key ways to encourage interests is through providing individuals with ample opportunities for exploration and discovery. This can involve exposing them to a wide range of activities, hobbies, and subjects, allowing them to find what truly captivates their attention. By offering a diverse array of experiences, individuals are more likely to stumble upon a passion that excites them and motivates them to delve deeper into a specific area.

Furthermore, offering support and guidance to individuals as they explore their interests is essential in nurturing their growth and development. This can involve providing resources, mentorship, and encouragement as they pursue their passions. By offering a helping hand along the way, individuals are more likely to overcome obstacles and challenges, allowing them to fully realize their potential and achieve their goals.

Promoting a growth mindset is also crucial in encouraging interests in individuals. By emphasizing the importance of perseverance, resilience, and continuous learning, individuals are more likely to push past their comfort zones and explore new possibilities. A growth mindset fosters a sense of curiosity and a willingness to take risks, which are essential qualities for developing and pursuing interests. By fostering curiosity and passion in various areas, individuals are able to discover their talents and strengths, leading to greater fulfillment and success in their lives. It is essential for educators, mentors, and leaders to prioritize the encouragement of interests in order to help individuals reach their full potential and achieve their goals.

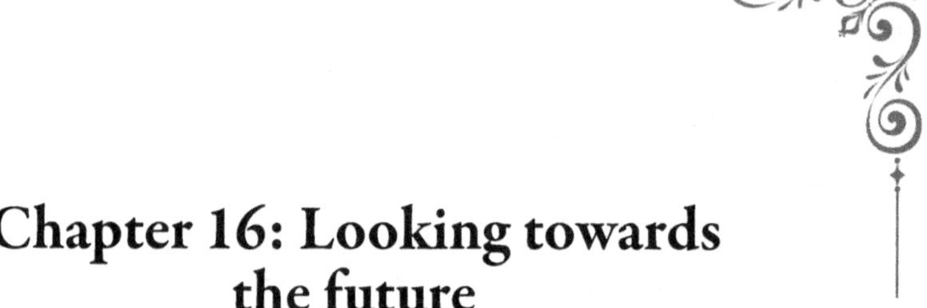

Chapter 16: Looking towards the future

- TRANSITIONING TO ADOLESCENCE

Adolescence is a significant period in the life of an individual, characterized by various physical, psychological, and social changes. The transition to adolescence is a crucial stage that marks the end of childhood and the beginning of adulthood. During this time, adolescents experience rapid growth and development, both physically and emotionally. It is a time of exploration and self-discovery, as they start to form their own identity and make decisions that will shape their future.

One of the key aspects of transitioning to adolescence is the physical changes that adolescents undergo. Puberty is a defining stage during which adolescents experience significant hormonal changes that lead to the development of secondary sexual characteristics. These changes can be unsettling for many adolescents, as they may feel self-conscious or insecure about their changing bodies. It is important for parents, educators, and other adults to provide support and guidance during this time, helping adolescents navigate these changes with confidence and self-acceptance.

In addition to physical changes, adolescents also experience significant cognitive and emotional developments during the transition to adolescence. This is a time when adolescents start to develop their own thoughts, beliefs, and values, independent of their parents or caregivers. They may question authority figures and challenge traditional norms and societal expectations. This period of self-discovery can be both exciting and challenging, as adolescents navigate their own identities and beliefs.

Socially, transitioning to adolescence involves developing relationships with peers and establishing a sense of belonging and acceptance within social groups. Adolescents may experience peer pressure to conform to certain behaviors or attitudes, which can be both positive and negative. It is important for adolescents to build strong social connections with peers who support and encourage their growth and development. Healthy peer relationships can provide a sense of belonging and acceptance, while also fostering personal growth and self-confidence.

During the transition to adolescence, adolescents may also face academic challenges as they navigate the increasing demands of school and extracurricular activities. This is a time when adolescents are expected to take on more responsibility for their own learning and academic success. It is important for parents, educators, and mentors to provide guidance and support to help adolescents develop effective study habits, time management skills, and problem-solving strategies. Encouraging adolescents to set realistic goals and work towards achieving them can help build their confidence and motivation to succeed academically. It is a time of exploration and self-discovery, as adolescents begin to form their own identity and make decisions that will shape their future. By providing support, guidance, and encouragement, adults can help adolescents navigate this period of transition with confidence and resilience. Adolescents who feel supported and empowered during this time are more likely to develop into healthy, confident, and successful adults.

- Planning for the future

Planning for the future is a critical aspect of personal and professional development. It involves setting specific goals, creating a roadmap to achieve those goals, and regularly reviewing and adjusting your plans based on changing circumstances. Without a clear plan for the future, individuals and organizations may struggle to achieve their desired outcomes and may find themselves adrift in a sea of uncertainty. By taking the time to carefully consider your long-term objectives and develop a strategic plan for achieving them, you can increase your chances of success and build a more secure and fulfilling future for yourself and those around you.

One of the key benefits of planning for the future is that it provides you with a sense of direction and purpose. By defining your goals and mapping out the steps needed to achieve them, you can create a clear vision of where you want to go and how you plan to get there. This sense of purpose can help you stay motivated and focused, even when faced with challenges or setbacks along the way. Without a clear plan in place, it can be easy to become overwhelmed by the uncertainties of the future and lose sight of your long-term objectives. By taking the time to carefully plan for the future, you can ensure that you are working towards meaningful and achievable goals that align with your values and priorities.

In addition to providing a sense of direction and purpose, planning for the future can also help you anticipate and prepare for potential obstacles and opportunities. By thinking ahead and considering different scenarios that may arise, you can develop contingency plans and strategies to mitigate risks and capitalize on opportunities as they present themselves. This proactive approach to planning can help you navigate the uncertainties of the future with greater confidence and resilience, knowing that you have thought through potential challenges and are prepared to respond accordingly. By developing a strategic plan for the future, you can position yourself to adapt and thrive in an ever-changing and unpredictable world.

Another key benefit of planning for the future is that it can help you make more informed and strategic decisions in the present. By having a clear understanding of your long-term goals and objectives, you can evaluate potential opportunities and challenges through the lens of how they align with your overall vision for the future. This can help you prioritize your time, resources, and energy on activities that will bring you closer to your goals and minimize distractions that may hinder your progress. By making decisions with your long-term objectives in mind, you can create a more intentional and purposeful approach to your personal and professional life, leading to greater satisfaction and success in the long run.

One of the key elements of effective planning for the future is setting specific, measurable, achievable, relevant, and time-bound (SMART) goals. By defining clear and actionable objectives that are aligned with your values and priorities, you can create a roadmap for success that guides your actions and decisions towards achieving your desired outcomes. SMART goals provide you with a framework for tracking your progress, measuring your success, and making adjustments as needed to stay on course. By breaking down your long-term goals into smaller, manageable milestones, you can create a sense of achievement and momentum that can fuel your motivation and drive towards reaching your ultimate objectives.

In addition to setting SMART goals, it is also important to regularly review and adjust your plans for the future based on changing circumstances and new information. The future is inherently unpredictable, and it is likely that your goals and priorities will evolve over time as you gain new insights and experiences. By taking the time to periodically assess your progress, reflect on your achievements and challenges, and adjust your plans as needed, you can ensure that you are staying on track towards your long-term objectives and remaining flexible and adaptable in the face of change. This process of ongoing planning and reflection can help you stay focused and aligned with your goals while also being responsive to new opportunities and challenges that may arise along the way. By setting specific goals, developing a strategic plan, and regularly reviewing and adjusting your plans based on changing circumstances, you can increase your chances of success and build a resilient and adaptive approach to navigating the uncertainties of the future. By taking the time to carefully consider your objectives, define your priorities, and develop a roadmap for achieving your goals, you can create a clear sense of direction and purpose that will guide your actions and decisions towards a brighter and more prosperous future.

- Supporting long-term goals

Supporting long-term goals is essential for achieving success and fulfillment in both our personal and professional lives. Long-term goals are the visions we have for our future, the aspirations and dreams that we work towards over an extended period of time. These goals require careful planning, dedication, and perseverance to accomplish. In order to support our long-term goals effectively, it is important to establish a clear understanding of what we want to achieve, break down our goals into manageable steps, and create a plan to stay motivated and focused along the way.

One of the first steps in supporting long-term goals is to clearly define what those goals are. This involves taking the time to reflect on our values, passions, and interests, and identifying the outcomes we hope to achieve in the future. By setting specific, measurable, achievable, relevant, and time-bound

(SMART) goals, we can create a roadmap for success that guides our actions and decisions. For example, if our long-term goal is to advance in our career and become a manager within the next five years, we could set specific milestones such as completing a leadership training program, gaining experience in cross-functional teams, and developing our communication skills to enhance our chances of promotion.

Once we have defined our long-term goals, the next step is to break them down into smaller, actionable steps. This process involves identifying the key tasks and milestones that need to be achieved along the way to reaching our ultimate goal. By breaking down our long-term goals into short-term objectives, we can create a sense of progress and momentum that keeps us motivated and on track. For example, if our long-term goal is to save enough money to buy a house in ten years, we could set short-term goals such as creating a budget, increasing our savings rate, and investing in long-term assets to generate passive income.

In addition to setting specific goals and breaking them down into manageable steps, it is important to create a plan that helps us stay focused and motivated over the long term. This involves establishing routines, habits, and systems that support our goals and hold us accountable for our actions. For example, if our long-term goal is to improve our physical fitness and run a marathon in two years, we could create a daily exercise schedule, meal plan, and tracking system to monitor our progress and stay committed to our goal. By creating a consistent routine and holding ourselves accountable for our actions, we can build the momentum and discipline needed to achieve our long-term goals. By setting clear goals, breaking them down into manageable steps, and creating a plan to stay focused and motivated, we can increase our chances of success and fulfillment in both our personal and professional lives. By taking the time to reflect on our values and aspirations, identify the outcomes we hope to achieve, and establish a roadmap for success, we can make progress towards our long-term goals and create a future that aligns with our dreams and ambitions. With dedication, perseverance, and a proactive approach to goal-setting, we can turn our long-term goals into reality and achieve the success and fulfillment we desire.

Chapter 17: Advocating for your child

- - - ❦ - - -

- UNDERSTANDING RIGHTS and laws

Rights and laws are essential components of any society, serving as the foundation for how individuals interact with one another and with the government. Understanding rights and laws is crucial for citizens to navigate their way through the complexities of legal systems and ensure that their rights are protected. In this essay, we will explore the concept of rights and laws, their importance in society, and how they work together to create a just and fair environment for all individuals.

Rights are fundamental entitlements that every individual possesses by virtue of being a human being. They are inherent and cannot be taken away or given up voluntarily. Rights can be divided into two broad categories: natural rights and legal rights. Natural rights, also known as human rights, are rights that are deemed universal and inalienable, such as the right to life, liberty, and property. Legal rights, on the other hand, are rights that are granted and protected by law, such as the right to free speech, the right to a fair trial, and the right to privacy.

Laws, on the other hand, are rules and regulations that are created by governments to govern the behavior of individuals and ensure order in society. Laws are enforced by the government through a system of courts and legal processes. Laws can be divided into different categories, such as criminal laws, civil laws, and administrative laws. Criminal laws govern offenses against the state, such as murder, theft, and assault. Civil laws govern disputes between individuals, such as contract disputes, property disputes, and family law matters. Administrative laws govern the actions of government agencies and officials.

Rights and laws work together to ensure that individuals are treated fairly and justly in society. Laws are created to protect and enforce rights, ensuring that individuals are able to exercise their rights without interference from others. For example, the right to free speech is protected by laws that prohibit censorship and limit government restrictions on speech. The right to a fair trial is protected by laws that establish rules and procedures for conducting trials and ensure that individuals are afforded due process and a fair hearing.

It is important for individuals to understand their rights and the laws that govern them in order to protect themselves and advocate for their interests. Understanding rights and laws allows individuals to navigate legal systems, assert their rights when they are violated, and seek redress through legal means. It also allows individuals to participate in the democratic process and hold governments accountable for upholding their rights and enforcing the law. Rights are fundamental entitlements that every individual possesses by virtue of being a human being, while laws are rules and regulations created by governments to govern the behavior of individuals and ensure order in society. Rights and laws work together to create a just and fair environment for all individuals, ensuring that they are treated fairly and justly in society. By understanding their rights and the laws that govern them, individuals can protect themselves, advocate for their interests, and hold governments accountable for upholding their rights and enforcing the law.

- Communicating with schools and professionals

Effective communication with schools and professionals is crucial for ensuring the success of students and achieving positive outcomes in various educational settings. Building strong relationships with schools and professionals can lead to collaboration, enhanced understanding, and improved support for students. In this article, we will explore the importance of communicating with schools and professionals, discuss key strategies for effective communication, and provide practical tips for improving communication in educational environments.

Developing strong communication channels with schools and professionals is essential for creating a supportive and conducive learning environment for students. By fostering positive relationships with schools and professionals, educators can gain valuable insights into the needs and challenges of their students, as well as access to valuable resources and support services. Effective communication can also help to build trust and mutual respect between educators and professionals, leading to improved collaboration and coordination of efforts to meet the diverse needs of students.

One key strategy for enhancing communication with schools and professionals is to establish clear and consistent lines of communication. This includes setting up regular meetings, phone calls, or email exchanges to discuss student progress, share information, and address any concerns or issues that may arise. By maintaining open and transparent communication channels, educators can promote a culture of collaboration and teamwork among all stakeholders involved in supporting student learning and development.

In addition to regular communication, it is important for educators to actively seek out feedback and input from schools and professionals to gain a better understanding of students' needs and how to best support them. This can be done through surveys, focus groups, or informal conversations to solicit input on strategies, programs, and interventions that can be implemented to improve student outcomes. By actively engaging with schools and professionals in this way, educators can demonstrate their commitment to continuous improvement and their willingness to work collaboratively to address the unique needs of their students.

Another important aspect of effective communication with schools and professionals is to ensure that information is clearly and accurately shared among all stakeholders. This includes using clear and concise language, providing relevant data and evidence to support claims or recommendations, and avoiding jargon or technical language that may be confusing or misunderstood. By communicating in a clear and accessible manner, educators can promote understanding and facilitate informed decision-making among all parties involved in supporting student success.

In addition to clear communication, it is also important for educators to be proactive in addressing any issues or concerns that may arise in their interactions with schools and professionals. This may involve identifying potential barriers to effective communication, such as conflicting schedules or miscommunication, and taking steps to address these issues to ensure that communication channels remain open and effective. By being proactive in addressing potential communication challenges, educators can prevent misunderstandings, conflicts, or breakdowns in communication that may hinder collaboration and coordination efforts.

Ultimately, it is important for educators to recognize the importance of building positive relationships with schools and professionals to support effective communication. This includes showing respect, empathy, and understanding towards all stakeholders, as well as valuing diverse perspectives and experiences. By building positive relationships based on trust, mutual respect, and a shared commitment to student success, educators can create a supportive and inclusive environment that fosters collaboration, teamwork, and innovation in addressing the diverse needs of students. By establishing clear and consistent lines of communication, seeking feedback and input, sharing information clearly and accurately, being proactive in addressing issues, and building positive relationships, educators can create a supportive and collaborative environment that promotes student learning and development. By following these key strategies and tips for effective communication, educators can enhance their interactions with schools and professionals, strengthen partnerships, and improve outcomes for all students.

- Ensuring access to accommodations

As educators and administrators, it is our responsibility to ensure that all students have access to the necessary accommodations to support their learning and success. This is especially important for students with disabilities, as they may require additional support to fully participate in educational activities. By providing accommodations, we can level the playing field and create a more inclusive and equitable learning environment for all students.

One key way to ensure access to accommodations is by implementing a comprehensive and thoughtful accommodation plan. This plan should be individualized and tailored to each student's specific needs and abilities. It should also take into account any relevant medical or psychological evaluations, as well as input from the student and their family. By working collaboratively with all stakeholders, including teachers, support staff, and outside professionals, we can create a plan that is realistic, effective, and sustainable.

Another important aspect of ensuring access to accommodations is by regularly assessing and monitoring the effectiveness of the accommodations provided. This can be done through ongoing communication with the student, their family, and any other relevant parties. By collecting data on the student's progress and adjusting accommodations as needed, we can ensure that they are receiving the support they need to succeed. Regular check-ins and evaluations can also help to identify any barriers or challenges that the student may be facing, and allow us to make adjustments accordingly.

In addition to individual accommodation plans, it is also important to create a school-wide culture of inclusivity and accessibility. This includes providing professional development opportunities for staff on best practices for accommodating students with disabilities, as well as ensuring that all school facilities and resources are accessible to students of all abilities. By fostering a culture of inclusion and understanding, we can create a more supportive and welcoming environment for all students.

Lastly, it is important to involve students in the accommodation process and empower them to advocate for their own needs. By encouraging students to speak up about the accommodations that work best for them, we can ensure that they are receiving the support that they require. This can also help to build self-advocacy skills and confidence in students, which can be beneficial both in school and beyond. By developing individualized accommodation plans, assessing their effectiveness, fostering a culture of inclusivity, and empowering students to advocate for their own needs, we can support students with disabilities in their academic and personal growth. It is our duty as educators and administrators to prioritize the needs of all students and provide them with the support they need to thrive. By working collaboratively and proactively, we can create a more accessible and inclusive educational experience for all.

Chapter 18: Connecting with other families

- SHARING EXPERIENCES

Sharing experiences is an essential aspect of human interaction and communication. It allows individuals to connect with one another, build relationships, and create a sense of community. By sharing our experiences with others, we not only learn from one another but also gain insights and perspectives that we may not have considered on our own. Whether it be talking about a recent vacation, recounting a personal triumph, or sharing a challenging experience, sharing our stories helps us to understand each other better and fosters a sense of empathy and understanding.

One of the key benefits of sharing experiences is the opportunity to learn from each other's successes and failures. When we share our experiences with others, we provide valuable insights and lessons that can help them navigate similar situations or challenges in their own lives. By sharing our struggles and triumphs, we can offer support and encouragement to those who may be going through similar experiences. This shared knowledge and wisdom can be incredibly valuable in helping others grow and learn from our own experiences.

In addition to learning from one another, sharing experiences also helps to create a sense of connection and belonging. When we share our experiences with others, we are inviting them into our world and allowing them to see us for who we truly are. This vulnerability and openness can foster deeper connections and strengthen relationships. By sharing our joys, sorrows, and struggles with others, we are opening ourselves up to their support, understanding, and compassion. This sense of connection and belonging is vital for our emotional well-being and can help us feel less alone in our experiences.

Furthermore, sharing experiences can also help to broaden our perspectives and challenge our assumptions. When we share our experiences with others, we are exposed to different viewpoints, beliefs, and values that may be different from our own. This exposure to diverse perspectives can help us broaden our understanding of the world and expand our worldview. By engaging in meaningful conversations and discussions with others, we can gain new insights and ideas that can challenge our existing beliefs and assumptions. This intellectual stimulation and exchange of ideas can help us grow and develop as individuals.

Another important aspect of sharing experiences is the opportunity for personal growth and self-reflection. When we share our experiences with others, we are forced to confront our own thoughts, emotions, and behaviors. This self-reflection can help us gain insight into our own strengths and weaknesses, as well as identify areas for growth and improvement. By sharing our experiences with others, we are inviting feedback, advice, and perspective that can help us become better versions of ourselves. This process of introspection and self-examination is essential for personal growth and development. By opening up and sharing our stories with others, we can create meaningful connections, broaden our perspectives, and challenge our assumptions. Through this process of shared experiences, we can gain valuable insights, support, and encouragement that can help us navigate life's challenges and triumphs. So, let us continue to share our experiences with one another, knowing that by doing so, we are building stronger relationships, fostering empathy, and creating a sense of community.

- Learning from others

Learning from others is a fundamental aspect of personal and professional growth. By observing and interacting with those around us, we have the opportunity to gain valuable insights, perspectives, and skills that can enhance our own knowledge and abilities. Whether it is through formal education, mentorship, or simply observing how others navigate challenges and opportunities, learning from others is a powerful way to expand our understanding and improve our own performance.

One of the key benefits of learning from others is the opportunity to gain new perspectives and approaches to problem-solving. When we interact with individuals who have different backgrounds, experiences, and ways of thinking, we are exposed to a diverse range of ideas and solutions that we may not have considered on our own. By engaging with others in meaningful conversations and collaborations, we can broaden our own thinking and expand our toolkit for addressing complex issues and challenges. In this way, learning from others can help us to develop more creative and effective strategies for success.

In addition to benefiting from new ideas and perspectives, learning from others can also provide us with valuable skills and knowledge that we may not have acquired through our own experiences. By observing how others approach tasks, communicate, and problem-solve, we can pick up on best practices and strategies that can help us to improve our own performance. Whether it is watching a colleague deliver a compelling presentation, a mentor navigate a difficult conversation, or a classmate excel in a particular subject, there is much to be gained from observing and learning from the behaviors and skills of those around us.

Furthermore, learning from others can also help us to build stronger relationships and networks that can support us in both our personal and professional lives. By actively engaging with others and seeking out opportunities to learn from their experiences and expertise, we can demonstrate our respect and appreciation for their knowledge and perspectives. This can help to create a sense of mutual trust and respect that can form the foundation for lasting and meaningful connections. By cultivating relationships with those who can mentor, advise, and support us, we can build a strong network of allies and mentors who can help us to navigate challenges, seize opportunities, and achieve our goals.

It is important to approach learning from others with an open mind and a willingness to be vulnerable and receptive to new ideas and perspectives. While it can be tempting to rely solely on our own experiences and knowledge, there is much to be gained from engaging with and learning from those around us. By embracing the opportunity to observe, listen, and engage with others, we can expand our own understanding, develop new skills, and build valuable relationships that can support us in our personal and professional growth. In this way, learning from others is an essential aspect of lifelong learning and development that can help us to continually improve and evolve as individuals.

- Building a supportive community

Building a supportive community is a crucial aspect of fostering positive social relationships and overall well-being among individuals. A supportive community provides a sense of belonging, acceptance, and safety for its members, which can lead to increased feelings of happiness and satisfaction in life. It is essential for community members to feel valued and respected by others, as this can help create a positive environment where individuals are encouraged to support and uplift one another.

One of the key components of building a supportive community is the establishment of strong communication channels among members. Effective communication is essential for understanding the needs and concerns of others, as well as for expressing one's own feelings and thoughts. By fostering open and honest communication, community members can develop a sense of trust and unity that is essential for building a supportive environment. Encouraging active listening and empathy can help create a culture of understanding and compassion within the community, which can strengthen relationships and create a sense of belonging for all members.

In addition to communication, building a supportive community also requires the promotion of inclusivity and diversity among its members. A supportive community should be a place where individuals from all backgrounds, cultures, and beliefs are welcomed and embraced. Embracing diversity can help create a more vibrant and dynamic community where different perspectives and experiences are valued and respected. By celebrating the unique qualities and contributions of each member, a supportive community can foster a sense of unity and collaboration that is essential for building strong social connections and relationships.

Another important aspect of building a supportive community is the promotion of mutual respect and kindness among its members. Respect and kindness are essential for creating a positive and nurturing environment where individuals feel safe and supported. Encouraging members to treat others with respect and kindness can help cultivate a culture of empathy and understanding within the community, which can strengthen relationships and create a sense of belonging for all members. By promoting a culture of mutual respect and kindness, a supportive community can create a sense of unity and camaraderie that is essential for fostering positive social relationships and overall well-being.

In order to build a supportive community, it is also important to create opportunities for members to connect and engage with one another. Organizing community events, group activities, and social gatherings can help bring members together and foster a sense of camaraderie and belonging. By providing opportunities for members to connect and form meaningful relationships, a supportive community can create a sense of unity and collaboration that is essential for building strong social connections and relationships. Encouraging members to participate in community events and activities can help create a sense of belonging and purpose for all members, which can lead to increased feelings of happiness and satisfaction in life.

Ultimately, building a supportive community requires a collective effort from all members to create a positive and nurturing environment where individuals feel valued, respected, and supported. By fostering open communication, promoting inclusivity and diversity, encouraging mutual respect and kindness, and creating opportunities for members to connect and engage with one another, a supportive community can provide a sense of belonging and acceptance for all its members. Through the collective efforts of its members, a supportive community can create a culture of empathy, understanding, and collaboration that is essential for fostering positive social relationships and overall well-being.

Chapter 19: Continued growth and development

- MONITORING PROGRESS

Monitoring progress is a critical component of any project or initiative, as it allows for the tracking of goals, objectives, and outcomes over time. By regularly monitoring progress, organizations can ensure that they are on track to achieve their desired outcomes and make any necessary adjustments to their plans as needed. This process involves collecting and analyzing data on various metrics and key performance indicators to assess how well a project is progressing towards its goals. It also involves communicating this information to stakeholders and team members to keep everyone informed and engaged in the process.

One of the key benefits of monitoring progress is that it provides organizations with valuable insights into the effectiveness of their strategies and tactics. By tracking key metrics and performance indicators, organizations can quickly identify areas where they are excelling and areas where they may be falling short. This allows them to make data-driven decisions about how to allocate resources, adjust timelines, or revise goals to ensure that they stay on track and achieve their desired outcomes. Without monitoring progress, organizations may find themselves working towards goals that are no longer relevant or realistic, which can waste time, money, and other resources.

Another important aspect of monitoring progress is the ability to track and measure the impact of a project or initiative over time. By collecting data on key performance indicators and other metrics, organizations can assess how well their efforts are achieving their intended outcomes. This can help them to identify areas where they may need to make changes or improvements to their strategies and tactics to enhance their effectiveness. By regularly monitoring progress, organizations can ensure that they are making the most of their resources and investments by focusing on activities that are generating the most impact.

Additionally, monitoring progress can help organizations to stay accountable to their stakeholders and other external audiences. By regularly reporting on progress towards goals and objectives, organizations can demonstrate their commitment to transparency and accountability. This can help build trust and confidence with stakeholders and other partners, who may be more likely to support and invest in future projects if they see evidence of progress and success. Monitoring progress also helps organizations to identify and address any challenges or obstacles that may be hindering their progress, which can help them to overcome these barriers and continue moving forward towards their goals. By collecting and analyzing data on key performance indicators and other metrics, organizations can gain valuable insights into the effectiveness of their strategies and tactics, measure the impact of their efforts, and stay accountable to stakeholders and other external audiences. By regularly monitoring progress and making data-driven decisions, organizations can ensure that they stay on track towards achieving their desired outcomes and making the most of their resources and investments.

- Celebrating milestones

Milestones are significant events or achievements that mark a significant point in one's journey or progress. These milestones can come in many forms, such as personal accomplishments, professional successes, or even important life events. Celebrating these milestones is important as it allows individuals to reflect on their accomplishments, feel a sense of pride and satisfaction, and motivate themselves to continue striving for success.

One of the key reasons why celebrating milestones is important is that it provides individuals with a sense of accomplishment and validation for their hard work and efforts. Achieving a milestone, whether it be a promotion at work, graduating from school, or reaching a personal goal, requires dedication, perseverance, and commitment. By taking the time to acknowledge and celebrate these achievements, individuals are able to recognize the value of their work and the progress they have made towards their goals. This sense of validation can boost self-confidence, improve self-esteem, and provide motivation to tackle future challenges with the same level of determination and drive.

In addition to providing a sense of accomplishment, celebrating milestones also allows individuals to reflect on their journey and the steps they have taken to reach their goals. It provides an opportunity for individuals to pause and appreciate the progress they have made, the obstacles they have overcome, and the lessons they have learned along the way. Reflecting on these experiences can help individuals gain a greater sense of self-awareness and perspective, as well as identify areas for growth and improvement. By taking the time to reflect on their journey, individuals can gain valuable insights that can inform their future decisions and actions, ultimately leading to continued growth and success.

Furthermore, celebrating milestones can also foster a sense of community and connection among individuals. Whether it be friends, family, colleagues, or mentors, sharing and celebrating achievements with others can strengthen relationships, build camaraderie, and create a sense of support and encouragement. Celebrating milestones with others allows individuals to feel seen, heard, and understood, and can instill a sense of belonging and interconnectedness. It can also serve as a source of inspiration and motivation for others, as they witness the success and achievements of their peers and feel encouraged to pursue their own goals and dreams.

Moreover, celebrating milestones can also serve as a way to set new goals, challenges, and aspirations for the future. By taking the time to acknowledge and celebrate their achievements, individuals can use this momentum as a springboard for setting new targets and objectives. Reflecting on past successes can help individuals gain a clearer sense of what they are capable of and what they can achieve in the future. It can also serve as a reminder of the importance of perseverance, determination, and hard work in reaching one's goals. By setting new milestones and challenges, individuals can continue to push themselves, grow, and evolve, ultimately leading to greater achievements and successes in the long run. By taking the time to celebrate these key moments, individuals can gain a sense of accomplishment, validation, and pride for their hard work and efforts. It also provides an opportunity for self-reflection, growth, and learning, as well as a chance to foster a sense of community and connection with others. By celebrating milestones, individuals can set new goals, challenges, and aspirations for the future, and continue on their journey towards success and fulfillment.

- Adjusting strategies as needed

Adjusting strategies as needed is a crucial aspect of effective decision-making and problem-solving in both personal and professional contexts. In any endeavor, unforeseen circumstances, changing market conditions, and evolving goals and objectives can necessitate a shift in approach or tactics. Being able to recognize when a strategy is no longer working or needs to be modified is a key skill that can lead to more successful outcomes. This process requires a combination of critical thinking, flexibility, and a willingness to adapt to new information and insights.

One of the primary reasons for adjusting strategies is the dynamic nature of the environment in which individuals and organizations operate. Whether it's in business, politics, or personal relationships, external factors can change rapidly and unexpectedly, necessitating a reevaluation of existing plans and tactics. For example, in the business world, a sudden shift in consumer preferences, new competitors entering the market, or changes in government regulations can all impact the effectiveness of a company's strategy. By regularly monitoring the external environment and staying informed about potential disruptors, decision-makers can proactively adjust their strategies to stay ahead of the curve.

Another reason for adjusting strategies is the realization that a current approach is not producing the desired results. This could be due to a variety of factors, such as inaccurate assumptions, flawed implementation, or unforeseen obstacles. In these situations, it is important to conduct a thorough analysis to determine the root cause of the problem and identify potential solutions. This may involve gathering feedback from stakeholders, conducting market research, or seeking guidance from experts in the field. By being open to feedback and willing to acknowledge when things are not going as planned, individuals and organizations can pivot to a new strategy that is more likely to achieve the desired outcomes.

Additionally, adjusting strategies may be necessary due to shifts in internal priorities, resources, or capabilities. As goals change, budgets fluctuate, or new technologies become available, it is important to reassess existing strategies to ensure they align with the organization's current objectives and capabilities. For example, if a company decides to prioritize sustainability initiatives, it may need to adjust its supply chain strategy, product offerings, or marketing messaging to reflect this new focus. By regularly reviewing internal resources and capabilities and aligning them with strategic goals, decision-makers can ensure that their strategies remain relevant and achievable.

In order to effectively adjust strategies as needed, decision-makers must adopt a flexible and agile mindset. This means being willing to let go of preconceived notions, experimenting with new approaches, and taking calculated risks. It also requires having the courage to admit when a strategy is not working and making the necessary adjustments, even if it means abandoning a previously held belief or course of action. By embracing a growth mindset and viewing challenges as opportunities for learning and improvement, individuals and organizations can foster a culture of adaptability and resilience.

Effective communication is also key to successfully adjusting strategies. Decision-makers must be able to clearly articulate the reasons for the change, the desired outcomes, and the steps required to implement the new strategy. This involves engaging with stakeholders, listening to their concerns and feedback, and building consensus around the need for change. By involving key players in the decision-making process and communicating openly and transparently, decision-makers can minimize resistance to change and ensure that everyone is on board with the new direction. By being proactive in monitoring external factors, recognizing when a strategy is not producing the desired results, and aligning internal priorities and capabilities with strategic goals, decision-makers can effectively adapt to changing circumstances and achieve their objectives. By fostering a culture of flexibility, agility, and open communication, individuals and organizations can navigate uncertainty and drive innovation and growth.

Chapter 20: Conclusion

- REFLECTING ON THE journey

Reflecting on the journey is a crucial part of personal growth and development. It allows individuals to pause, look back on their experiences, and gain valuable insights into their successes, challenges, and areas for improvement. By taking the time to reflect, individuals can deepen their self-awareness, refine their goals, and make better decisions moving forward. Reflecting on the journey is not just about reminiscing on past events; it is about actively engaging with one's experiences, emotions, and thoughts to gain a deeper understanding of oneself and one's path.

One of the key benefits of reflecting on the journey is the opportunity to celebrate one's successes and accomplishments. By looking back on the steps taken, obstacles overcome, and goals achieved, individuals can acknowledge their hard work and perseverance. This acknowledgment boosts confidence and motivation, reinforcing the belief in one's abilities to tackle future challenges. Celebrating successes also provides a sense of fulfillment and satisfaction, reminding individuals of their capacity for growth and achievement.

Reflecting on the journey also offers an opportunity to identify areas for improvement and growth. By examining past mistakes, failures, and shortcomings, individuals can pinpoint patterns or behaviors that may be holding them back. This reflection allows for self-correction and learning, paving the way for personal development and progress. It is important to approach these areas with curiosity and compassion, reframing them as opportunities for growth rather than sources of shame or regret. Embracing these challenges as learning experiences can lead to greater self-awareness and resilience.

In addition to celebrating successes and identifying areas for growth, reflecting on the journey can also help individuals clarify their values, priorities, and goals. By examining past choices and experiences, individuals can gain clarity on what truly matters to them and what they want to achieve in the future. This reflection provides a solid foundation for setting meaningful and achievable goals that align with one's values and aspirations. It can also help individuals make more informed decisions and take purposeful actions that are in line with their personal vision for the future.

Moreover, reflecting on the journey fosters a sense of gratitude and appreciation for the people, experiences, and opportunities that have shaped one's path. By acknowledging the support, guidance, and contributions of others along the way, individuals can cultivate a sense of connection and community. Expressing gratitude not only strengthens relationships but also nourishes a positive outlook and mindset. It is important to recognize the impact of others on one's journey and to express gratitude for the resources and support that have been instrumental in personal growth and development. By celebrating successes, identifying areas for improvement, clarifying values and goals, and expressing gratitude, individuals can gain valuable insights into their experiences and chart a path forward that is meaningful and fulfilling. This reflective process requires time, effort, and commitment, but the rewards are profound and can pave the way for a more purposeful and authentic life. Embracing the journey with an open heart and mind allows individuals to learn from the past, live in the present, and envision a brighter future filled with growth, connection, and possibility.

- Looking towards the future

The future holds significant promise and potential for innovation across a variety of industries and sectors. As we look towards what lies ahead, it is essential to consider the technological advancements, demographic shifts, and global challenges that will shape our future landscape. In today's rapidly evolving world, the pace of change is accelerating, and it is more important than ever to stay ahead of the curve and adapt to new trends and developments.

One of the key drivers of change in the future will be advancements in technology. From artificial intelligence and machine learning to virtual reality and blockchain, the possibilities for innovation are endless. As these technologies become more integrated into our daily lives, they will revolutionize the way we work, communicate, and interact with the world around us. Companies that embrace these technologies and incorporate them into their business strategies will have a competitive edge in the future marketplace.

Another important factor to consider as we look towards the future is the shifting demographic landscape. With an aging population and increasing diversity, businesses will need to adapt their practices to cater to a changing customer base. Understanding the needs and preferences of different demographic groups will be critical for success in the future. Companies that prioritize diversity and inclusion will not only be better equipped to serve their customers but will also attract top talent and enhance their brand reputation.

In addition to technological advancements and demographic shifts, the future will also bring about global challenges that will require innovative solutions. From climate change and sustainable development to geopolitical tensions and economic inequalities, there are a host of complex issues that will need to be addressed in the years to come. Companies that take a proactive approach to these challenges and incorporate sustainability and social responsibility into their business practices will be well-positioned to thrive in the future.

As we look towards the future, it is clear that change is inevitable. By staying informed, adopting a growth mindset, and embracing new opportunities, individuals and organizations can navigate the uncertain terrain ahead with confidence and resilience. The key to success in the future will be adaptability and agility, as well as a willingness to think outside the box and explore unconventional solutions. By fostering a culture of innovation and collaboration, we can create a future that is brighter, more inclusive, and more sustainable for generations to come.

- Celebrating successes

Celebrating successes is an essential aspect of personal and professional growth. Whether it be a small achievement or a major milestone, taking the time to acknowledge and celebrate our successes can have a significant impact on our overall well-being and motivation. By recognizing and honoring our accomplishments, we not only boost our self-esteem and confidence but also foster a positive and rewarding mindset that can propel us forward in our journey towards success.

One of the key reasons why celebrating successes is important is that it serves as a powerful motivator. When we take the time to acknowledge and celebrate our achievements, we are reinforcing positive behavior and encouraging ourselves to continue striving for more. By celebrating our successes, we are essentially rewarding ourselves for our hard work and dedication, which can help to keep us motivated and focused on our goals. This positive reinforcement can be a powerful tool in driving us towards even greater accomplishments in the future.

Another benefit of celebrating successes is that it helps to build resilience and fortitude. In the face of challenges and setbacks, it can be easy to become discouraged and lose sight of our goals. However, by taking the time to celebrate our successes, no matter how small they may seem, we are reminding ourselves of our capabilities and strengths. This can help to boost our resilience and fortitude, allowing us to better navigate obstacles and setbacks that may come our way. By acknowledging and celebrating our achievements, we are building a foundation of confidence and self-belief that can help us to overcome challenges and continue moving forward.

Celebrating successes also creates a sense of accomplishment and fulfillment. When we take the time to reflect on our achievements and celebrate our successes, we are instilling a sense of pride and fulfillment in ourselves. This sense of accomplishment can be incredibly rewarding and can help to boost our overall sense of well-being and satisfaction. By acknowledging and celebrating our successes, we are honoring our hard work and dedication, which can foster a greater sense of purpose and fulfillment in our lives.

Moreover, celebrating successes can also help to foster a positive and supportive work culture. When individuals and teams take the time to acknowledge and celebrate their achievements, it can create a sense of camaraderie and unity. By recognizing and honoring the successes of others, we are fostering a culture of support and encouragement that can help to build strong and cohesive teams. Celebrating successes can also help to boost morale and motivation within a team, creating a positive and collaborative work environment where individuals feel valued and appreciated. By taking the time to acknowledge and honor our achievements, we can boost our motivation, build resilience, create a sense of accomplishment and fulfillment, and foster a positive and supportive work culture. Whether it be a small victory or a major milestone, celebrating successes is an important practice that can help to propel us forward in our journey towards success. So, let us take the time to acknowledge and celebrate our achievements, to honor our hard work and dedication, and to build a foundation of confidence and self-belief that will help us to achieve even greater feats in the future.